Red Star
Over Hebrides

Donald S Murray

First published by Taproot Press 2023
ISBN: 978-1739207717
The author's right to be identified as author of this book under
the Copyright, Designs and Patents Act 1988 has been asserted.
Printed and bound by Totem, Inowroclaw, Poland
Typeset in 11.5 point Adobe Garamond Pro by Ryan Vance
Cover design: Mark Mechan
© Donald S Murray 2023

CONTENTS

*To the people of South Dell, Ness, Isle of Lewis
whose stories formed the basis of this work,
and to Maggie Priest, Patrick Jamieson
and Calum Ferguson, who encouraged me
to build on these foundations.*

FOREWORD

The obvious difference between living in the Isle of Lewis and locations like Russia, Poland, Ukraine and Belarus is the thickness of the landscape in which people existed both now and in the past.

Yet strangely enough, it might have been exactly that – the contrast between the narrowness of the strip of land on which we lived and the huge, open spaces of the former Soviet Union – which generated such an interest in that country when I grew up in my native district of Ness in the sixties and early seventies.

There was no doubt that several people both in my village and elsewhere possessed a fascination for 'Russian' literature. There were a few who spoke to me about that nation's literary skills when I was young—mainly members of the Campbell family who lived nearby. They talked about the power and potency of writers like Dostoevsky, Tolstoy and Solzhenitsyn; one of them even handing me a copy of *Crime and Punishment* long before I was old enough to appreciate it. 'See if you can read that,' he said. I couldn't. But it prepared the way for studying texts like Solzhenitsyn's *One Day in the Life of Ivan Denisovich* and *Cancer Ward* in my final years in school.

This interest in Russia might have been sparked by the political. After the First World War, a number of land-raids took place in the islands. The nearest to my home village of South Dell was neighbouring Galson, which had been a farm for years before a number of men from both the district of Ness and other locations such as Borve and Shader reclaimed it as their own, transforming its wide fields into croftland. In doing this, people cited the Government's promises of land for those who had conscripted as the reason for their actions.

There were, however, other motivations, including the example of the Russian Revolution in 1917. This, too, inspired individuals to imitate those across the former Russian empire who claimed the territory formerly possessed by their landlords as their own—even if this was very different from the traditions of these islands in the way these acres were part of a 'collective ownership' under Soviet rule. Instead the majority of crofters wanted a degree of independent control, even if outside the boundaries of Stornoway and some of its nearby villages, their land was still part of a distantly owned estate.[1]

Even before the First World War, there was some 'Russian' influence. Fishing boats from St Petersburg and Riga – in modern day Latvia – used to arrive at Stornoway Harbour or other small ports in the Western Isles, bringing fish from these waters to feed the multitude who lived under Tsarist control. The collapse of this market following the Revolution had a huge economic effect on the Western Isles. The fishing boats there could

1   The Stornoway area and the villages of the north-eastern end of the island were under community ownership, becoming part of a community trust in 1923, a hundred years ago. The situation in Lewis has changed in recent years, with a number of other districts following this example not only in that island but in other communities like South Uist and Harris.

no longer sell their catch to those who lived locally or to Germany. Oddly this market once again came to life in the seventies—a time when I can recall 'Russian' ships either anchored near Stornoway or in greater numbers off Ullapool on the west coast of the Highlands. One of the highlights of my late teenage years was seeing 'Russian' and 'Polish' notices sellotaped to shop windows in that small town, limiting the number of visitors from these parts stepping within their doors. Even despite this, there were whispers. I recall discovering that Rumania was the most repressive of all the Eastern European states, with every movement of the fishermen on board that nation's ships being closely watched by those on board.

Given the strength of religious belief in my native district at that time, it is also not inconceivable that many who were drawn to a spiritual life found much of interest in the works of Dostoevsky, Tolstoy and others, especially in the way these authors asked challenging moral and ethical questions of their readers. This is true even of the works of Solzhenitsyn, another writer to whom the Christian faith was also important.

Peculiarly, too, it may also have appealed to those who had the opposite view. There were some who found living in the Presbyterian environment of islands like Lewis extremely repressive and harsh, especially on a Sunday. Reading some of these authors may have helped individuals with that mindset to cope with the strains and stresses of life in a society dominated by the Church and its leaders. They would lay these books down with the thought 'we are not alone' uppermost in their minds.

Looking back at my own childhood, there were some advantages in the way Sabbath Observance affected the islands. I was not allowed to watch TV on Sunday. Instead, my father—a church elder who was more 'liberal' than many of his ilk—encouraged me to read widely. It was during these times I first learned to love the work of the Ukrainian writer, Gogol, Czech novelists and storytellers like Kafka and—later—Kundera and a horde of other East European writers, such as Gorky, Sholokhov, Bulgakov and Bruno Schulz's *Street of Crocodiles*. Noting my fondness for reading stories about events far beyond our island shores, my father used to order the US magazine *Newsweek* for me to read most weekends. While I became very quickly aware of the propaganda element that was part of that publication, it still fascinated me. I remember particularly its coverage of the situation in Poland, especially the struggle between Lech Walesa and the Solidarity movement against the Communist government. Part of this interest was generated because it was a country I had often heard discussed in my childhood home. My father and uncles had all worked alongside 'Poles' in the creation of hydro dams across the Highlands. I even recall my father reliving that experience and reminding someone in a conversation.

'They weren't all Poles. Some of them were Ukrainians.'

Perhaps these words, too, played their part in the creation of the book that follows. It was as if the Minch that divided Lewis from the rest of Scotland opened up when I heard them, making it possible for me not only to cross these narrow waters but also to step towards the North Sea and the Baltic, allowing me a little peek behind the Iron Curtain—even if it was only in my imagination.

Together with my interest in Gaelic song as a child and teenager, this book is a product of the journey I took at that time.

Donald S Murray

*'All our thinking, our looking
and our reading was governed
during those years by an obsession
with allusion. Each word brought another
one to mind; each had a double meaning,
a false bottom, a hidden significance;
each contained something secretly encoded,
cunningly concealed ...'*

'Travels with Herodotus'
Ryszard Kapuscinski

Prelude
MOTHER RUSSIA

I can see these islands mirror Russia.
The machair's sweep reflect the steppes
while moors multiply tenfold,
transformed into tundra,
with houses squat in Arctic winds
that shake the fragile edges
of both tree and man.

And the people, too,
clinging to the orthodoxies of Kirk or State
or singing songs sonorous with sadness—
the Volga boatmen crossing seas
to Mingulay;
some cailleach's coat
covering Krushchev or Cherenkov's wife;
Yeltsin reeling through the Kremlin
or the council chamber's doors;
Vlad bare-chested on the machair
with a fishing rod in hand.

MOSCOW FOLK STATE BALLAD 1957
(inspired by 'MacArthur Park')

Someone left the drink out in the train
for Harris and the Lewisman to swallow
all the way from Paris through to Moscow
where they went off the rails again

and stepped into that Russian city's rain
booming out Irish and Gaelic songs,
pretending each wheelbarrow now belonged
to Molly, or that their drink-befuddled brains

could see the 'Bratach Bana' tied up at the Kremlin.
'Stalin mo rùin-sa', 'Mountain dew',
each chorus following them as they stepped through
Solyanka Street or round the Garden Ring,

aware that as they stumbled in the dark
that both sky and skin were melting
and they would have to find some space within
a near hotel, where their teetering bones might park.

LENINGRAD 1960

Kenneth felt more weedlike than ever, as if he were a blur of green and blue about to be chopped by the giant sickles looming above his head. The shade of his face had much in common with the flags that seemed to hang everywhere too. His nervousness grew even greater as a dancing girl – the one introduced to him earlier as Nuriya – approached him behind the stage, her smile wide and gleaming.

'Can I touch?' she whispered, stretching out her hand.

'Uh ... of course.'

'This is beautiful.' She fingered his plaid. 'Tell me. Is everything in the West as beautiful as this?'

He trembled, only too aware that the girl suited that particular adjective far more than his Mackenzie tartan. There was her long dark hair, high cheekbones, wide brown eyes, bright and exotic clothes. Dressed in what he had been told was a Tatar dancing costume, she wore a black pillar box hat studded with pearls, a veil draping down her back, a tight crimson bodice emphasising the curve of her breasts.

'Not everything ...' he muttered.

'No?'

'But the place I come from is ...' he said, thinking of the hills, bays and beaches near his home. His memory of their presence seemed unreal as he stood waiting to sing in the Gorky Theatre in Leningrad with its huge banner of Khrushchev's face hanging from the ceiling, the words, *Life has become better, life is more joyful* printed – or so he had been told – below.

'And where is that?'

'Harris. It's an island off the coast.'

But he never had the chance to tell her exactly where it was. He was interrupted by Dmitri, a broad, burly man with a dark moustache and a Marx pin in the lapel of his jacket.

'It is nearly your turn, Kenneth.'

Kenneth nodded, his mouth drying as it always did before a performance. He was listening to the Master of Ceremonies talk in English, speaking of how much their former leader, Comrade Lenin, had loved music. In his younger days, apparently, he used to sing 'The Internationale' while his sister, Olga, played piano. During the dark days of the civil war, he had always asked, 'What are the young people singing? Let me know what songs they are choosing.'

'It is clear from all this that Comrade Lenin knew the importance of music, how it is a touchstone for us all. It is for this reason that we, the Central Soviet of this fine city bearing his name, decided to initiate the Lenin People's Award for Music. One of its first winners is a young man from the islands off the coast of Scotland, a singer of a language – Scottish Gaelic – that the reactionary bourgeois elements in that country have long attempted to repress and silence. My fellow comrades, I present to you Kenneth Mackenzie ...'

He flexed his fingers before stepping on stage.

Pausing at its centre, he was still as he gazed into the lights, silent until the applause died away. When he spoke, his voice faded to a whisper.

'This is a song about something that is a long way from you here in Leningrad. The power of the sea. Ladies and gentlemen, 'An Ataireachd Ard'.'

It was only after the music entered nerve and muscle that he began to sing.

'An ataireachd bhuan,
Cluinn fuaim na h-ataireachd ard ...'

His eyes scanned the audience as the notes eased out, loud and strong. He had watched them since his arrival at the theatre—those men with dark suits, soft felt hats; their wives red-cheeked and overweight. Wrapped in thick coats, their clothes offered no crack or crevice for the Russian winter to peek its way through. With the exception of a few members of the military, an Astrakhan hat or two, it was easy to pretend they were a congregation of the Free Church back home—except that their like would never have stepped into a hall, not to listen to Kenneth and his devil's gift of song. Such a notion would have been unthinkable to them.

The Russians, however, took to him with enthusiasm. This was no threatening agent of the West, but instead, a pale, fragile youth with tortoise-shell glasses, a tight knot of fair curls. He looked more angel than capitalist demon with that wing of tartan on his shoulder, white knees braving the theatre's cold.

'Now my first song was about the ocean. My next is about one of the vessels that travel on it. Called 'Bratach

Bana', it tells a simple story, of the sighting of a tall, white-sailed ship on the horizon …'

He heard their hands and feet beat to the rhythm of the music, the entire hall sailing on its flow. The words of Antonio, his music teacher during his year in Glasgow, came into his head. Quoting Goethe, he had declared, 'Such is the price the gods exact for song, to become what we sing.' He knew exactly what that meant. He had become purely a voice, escaping the awkwardness that plagued the rest of him whenever a pretty girl came near, made speechless even by her mere existence.

'My last song is about a dark period in our history. It tells of how the people of the islands were cleared from their land and taken on tall ships – just like the 'Bratach Bana' – into exile in Canada. It was a place they hated. They called it the 'choille gruamach'—the gloomy forest, a land where snow and ice made the soil hard and impenetrable for much of the year. One of our Gaelic poets, Iain MacGhille-eathain, composed this song about his years there, his longing for the land he had left.

'Gu bheil mi am onrachd 'sa choille ghruamaich
Mo smaointean luaineach, cha tog mi fonn …'

'Perfection is our only duty,' one of the Russians had told him, 'It is what we all must aim for.' And he touched it with his voice that night, knowing that his audience was with him, aware, too, of the ovation they would reward him with at the song's end. When that came, he would leave the stage reluctantly, returning a short while later for the inevitable encore ...

'Well done, Kenneth.' A man from Finland shook his hand almost as vigorously as he had pumped his accordion earlier that evening. 'That was excellent.'

'Congratulations. Our ambassador was right. You have an excellent voice.'

'Well done.'

'It is good to know that the thaw has finally come. Even at this time of year. Your voice heralds a new Russian spring. A new time of peace between our countries.'

'Wonderful. Wonderful. Wonderful.'

Even the policeman who stood near the stage doorway joined in, slapping his shoulder. Kenneth smiled thinly in response, aware that such words were usually meat and drink to him. Praise. Pats on the back. The clasp of fingers. They allowed him to escape his shyness, his sense of being lost within the world. Yet that night, he felt more awkward and clumsy than ever. Looking round for Nuriya, he discovered that she was one of those performing on stage. A Tatar dance. With others around her, she twirled and reeled to the music, moving under bridges shaped by the arms and smiles of young men and women, all dressed in similar clothes. They sank to their knees and then rose, shouted and clapped their hands before dropping to their knees once more. One girl crossed her legs and kicked.

And then just as Kenneth thought they were finished, Nuriya stepped out. Her hands were placed firmly on her hips, thumbs tucked at her back. She moved towards the floor. Squatting, her legs kicked out again and again, shifting in time to the speed of the rhythm.

'Yyyyyiiiiyyyaaaaa!'

He admired her grace and energy, how in her own way she had done what Goethe had spoken about, becoming one with song. For once, he felt he had come across someone who was very much like him. The spirit of his islands merging with the spirit of the steppes or Volga or wherever on earth she came from. She had become the dance, her breasts, legs, thighs as much part of the flow of music as the musicians who played behind her.

He waited until she finished, wrapping his arms around her, rejoicing in her applause.

'Nuriya. That was wonderful.'

'No. No. Not good. You were excellent, Kenneth. I was …'

'Nuriya. That isn't true. You were amazing.'

'No. No. That song you sung. It was wonderful. So true. So sad.'

He allowed her to escape his hold, sensing that she wanted to talk. He saw once again her dark brown eyes, scarlet lips, her breasts heaving.

'That song you sang. It told about my people, the Tatars. How they were taken by Stalin from their homes in the Crimea. How they were scattered all over, sent to our – how you say – gloomy forests in the east. And many were killed. Many. Many.'

He drew away, alarmed by her words.

'Sorry?'

'Your words. They spoke to me about my people. The Tatars. How they were treated. How they were killed.'

His head felt dizzy. Empty. Ignorant.

'But it's just a song,' he muttered. 'A song. About something that happened a hundred years ago.'

'No. No. I was young when this happened. Not so long ago. I can remember how we were forced into lorries, taken away. My father murdered. Shot. Thrown into a ditch.' She stammered even more than he sometimes did, frightened and scared. 'Kenneth … I shall come to your room tonight. Tell you more about it. Sleep with you.'

'Sorry?'

'Yes. Yes. I will let you sleep with me. Perhaps if I please you, you will take me away with you. To the West. Maybe? Maybe?'

He was aware of her breasts against him, how her closeness was making him giddy—his body hot and sweating for all that the building was chilled and icy, snowflakes reeling through the dark street outside. He was conscious, too, of how little her words were making sense to him. They seemed remote and distant, having no connection with his understanding of the world.

'If that is too much to ask, perhaps, you will take a note and some photos with you. To tell the West about the things happening to my people. For all that, I will sleep with you. Just for that.'

Again, he could not speak, aware only of his own lack of knowledge, how little he knew of this place with its pictures of Marx and Lenin, its letters as sharp and angular as barbed wire. And now there was this woman offering herself to him, acting in a way he had never seen a girl behave before.

'Kenneth?'

He looked up to see Dmitri coming towards him, his guide's face dark and troubled. He spoke the same word as Nuriya had used just a moment before.

'Kenneth.'

Nuriya's arms withdrew. He felt the tautness of her body loosen and give way.

'Kenneth. Is there anything the matter?'

'N-n-no.' He shook his head.

Dmitri knew he was lying. The Russian pulled Nuriya away. Words barbed his lips, almost as rough and fierce as the hand that pushed her across the floor, tunic bunched inside his fist.

'Sorry, Kenneth. Sorry,' she kept saying, her eyes wide and frightened. 'Sorry for the trouble I have caused you.'

'No more,' Dmitri said in English. 'No more talk.'

He bundled Nuriya towards the policeman who had congratulated Kenneth a short time before. The singer watched as the girl was grabbed and thrust out of the back door he was guarding—into the Leningrad streets or the back of a police van. For a moment, he saw the whirl of snowflakes, a flickering lamp outside. Then the door slammed behind her. The noise stilled and stifled conversation for a long time before voices dared to speak once again.

'You are Scotsman. With kilt. You are magnificent singer. Comprehendez?' a stranger said.

'My wife and I. We love your music. We love your music.'

Finally, words began to form. He spat his questions at Dmitri's back, spluttering in the darkness of the theatre.

'Where did he take her? What the hell's going to happen to her?'

When Dmitri finally turned round to answer him, he was smiling once again—his grin as bright and intimidating as the gleam of his Marx pin.

'No questions. It was nothing,' he said. 'Nothing that need concern a singer. Nothing that need trouble him at all.'

SKIGERSTA

1

When that fisherman came to purchase ling
in Skigersta, he used to bring
eggs from the Tsar or King

of fish so they could feast.
'A gift,' he said, 'from far-off east.'
Its dark taste released

dreams of wolves and boars
she'd never witnessed on these shores.
Men in bearskins, priests who wore

great hats and carried a gold cross.
Until the War came and he was lost,
visiting her only in her thoughts,

as if the sledge had been trapped
by snow and ice, an avalanche
men had slipped to block the path

their boats had sailed for centuries past,
from Lewis northwards to Murmansk.

2

When Pyotr walked the moor near Skigersta,
he recalled the wide stretch of the tundra

and looked out for sign of wolves and bears
he thought might still flourish there.

But none could be found—not even hares
that altered shade in winter. He'd go back and declare

these barren acres barely fit to feed
the rancid flocks of sheep

that grazed there, enticing women with his talk
of sable, fox-fur, bearskin to wrap them in the dark

of his home, his bare shoulders, too, providing warmth
on nights when the fire sank

when air seeped cold and dank

3

She'd seen a card once that pictured
a snow-whiskered man
perched upon a sleigh
and imagined there were others just like him
in that country, far away
who might take her from this island where salt winds
    scathed her cheeks
and made her shake and tremble,
crunch her bottom lip,

to exchange all this for a green glade where she'd find
shelter among pines
surrounding her like heather—
tall and thick and kind

where each day she might pretend to sit
like that whitebeard
in her sleigh-seat,
circled by a horde of gifts.

4

For years the names of unfamiliar places
had occasionally brushed their lips,
sounds like Manitoba, Winnipeg, Ontario,
becoming familiar when ships

had taken relatives to foreign shores.
But these were different kinds of words,
jumbles of sounds and syllables
they'd never dreamed or heard

before. More obscure even than English
most had tried to learn at school.
Psalms and catechisms recited.
Yards and furlongs. Multiplication rules

belted deep within their heads.
And now these ports and towns
they'd never imagined.
They felt surrounded by the sounds

of these locations mentioned in their speech.
Marooned in Murmansk or Moscow.
Locations far beyond their reach.

5

One night they spoke of railways
and how their country was criss-crossed by tracks
which carried fish to market,
brought citizens there and back

from shores that were familiar far inland.
It made her dream of swathes of land
as huge as waves criss-crossing the Atlantic
a few miles close to hand,

and how she might glimpse different skies
through the broken wood-slats
of the wagon that she crouched inside
while the train tugged them across the flat

acres of the steppes,
its engine like a heartbeat, one that stirred
her like the loud click-clack of consonants
she sometimes heard within his words.

Not like the tongue with which her neighbours spoke,
voices that—for so long—had marked the world
in which her life was tied and snarled.

6

The hull had been glazed with ice a few times,
locals noted while examining the boat.
Cabin scratched and scarred by frost.
They wondered how it stayed afloat

under the weight of snow
or crashed its way towards their coastline.
She took its coming as an omen,
a portent that lives were to be aligned,

like fate had opened a gate
for its arrival across the Pentland Firth
and Minch, the North Sea,
churning channels through the waters of the earth

to take that man close towards her,
and offer her release
from the borders of the island,
the confinement that she'd suffered since her birth.

7

They burst out laughing at the village kirk,
comparing it to those at home.
No bell-tower high upon its slated roof.
No spire. No shaped or rounded dome.

And then they heard the psalms peal out
behind its grey and wind-scoured walls,
spiralling high into the heavens,
a chorus that both rises, falls,

until it spills out to encompass fields
of oats and grass edging to the shore,
plaiting voices like the sheaves
they'd passed, a harvest for the soul.

8

One of the neighbours asked them
what it was like to live under the Tsar.
They pretended not to hear them, fearing
their response might echo far
from Skigersta or Lewis,
in Vilnius
or perhaps Murmansk,
whichever port from which they sailed,
crows or gulls might hear and pass
their answers on to those who might seal
them in a Labour camp or jail.
Even though the only witnesses
were seabirds or a sheep,
who knew what a ram or ewe might bleat one day,
or what secret a beak might fail to keep?

9

The depths between the Butt and Cape Wrath rang
with the notes of the balalaika
as one of the fishermen sang
the anthem of the boatmen on the Volga,

and how they hauled and tugged their oars
past Volograd and Astrakhan
reservoirs, plains and shores,
so different from the cliffs and moors that surrounded them

on this small harbour here.
Yet locals recognised the beat
and rhythm of that music,
how songs like this one granted cheer

when they tugged and veered
around the narrow waters of the Minch,
allowing notes to strengthen them
as they moved forward inch by earnest inch.

10

Nights when they were anchored there,
the moon circled close,
perching on the peninsula of Point,
crouching on the coastline of Sutherland,

as if its light was furred
with the animals they spoke about
while sitting around the samovar
with pelts of wolves,
hide of bears
cloaking the lunar landscape,
a blur

on contours seen
throughout her life.
Instead, she saw the Minch
glittering with lines

which allowed beasts of prey
rights of entrance to forbidden shores
long guarded by wild waters,
finding new ways to explore

length and stretch, gaining sustenance
from all they could find to feast upon,
the carcasses of whales and seals
washed up and broken on the beach.

11

There was a legend, one man said,
he'd heard way back in Saaremaa,
that the Northern Lights above their heads
were horses pulling a silver chariot
when ancient Gods were wed.

She dreamed that night while these lights danced,
each beam lively, quick, and agile,
that she might one day have the chance
to imitate their sparkle
and add her own gleam to these northern skies,
rejoicing in their broad expanse.
And she moved closer to the man who'd spoken,
believing some spark passed
between them
creating its own aurora,
its silver chariot of romance.

12

She broke the surface of the well
and dipped her pail deep within cold water.
A scattering of ice. A crack within the storm
like when her father looked after

ewes shrouded by snow upon their croft.
A different chill surrounded her, one she tried to crack
open that cold morning she stepped upon the boat
to go and meet him in the damp and dark.
When she slipped on board that vessel,
she knew there would never be a way of turning back.

13

He whispered to her that she bore the name of queens.
'Catriona ... Catherine. Just like him. The new Peadair
the Great.'
They could be monarchs of all that they surveyed
whether this was heather or the steppes.

She would hold her hand outstretched
for men to kiss and kneel.
A fantasy, she knew, but nothing wrong
with having dreams.

Sometimes they kept
a woman upright when hauling pails of water from the well.
Or gutting fish. She smelled the incense in cathedrals

each time he spoke to her.
The icons on windows, walls,
an escape from the bare and horizontal
in all the tales she heard him tell,

relief from the smell
of peat-smoke
that choked her in the blackhouse where her parents dwelled.

14

There was no horse in Skigersta.
Not even when neighbours ploughed and farmed
each damp and stony slice of ground.
Perhaps they were alarmed

by these fishermen's talk of Cossacks
high upon their saddles bearing arms
against all who dared to speak
or whisper against the Tsar.

Perhaps, too, they saw each horse as heralding
the Apocalypse, bringing harm
and guarding themselves against the hooves
with prayers and slowly rendered psalms.

15

One man swooned under the swirl of spirits
these fishermen carried with them on their boat,
transforming green ridges into great waves,
trying hard to stay afloat.

The next day he awoke,
bones chilled as the tundra
of which these visitors had sometimes spoken,
his head full of smack and thunder

of the sea. He thought he'd been transported
to a camp near Vladivostok,
his neighbours plunging him into exile
on a vessel launched from island rocks.

16

'*Napoleon's troops got bogged down*
in snow and sleet, marsh and rock-strewn land that surrounds
the edge of Moscow,' the old schoolmaster said.
'*Soon they all retreated, scrambling over the crippled and*
the dead

to get back to the border they'd marched over months before.
No food for them to eat. The Russian soldiers had prepared
for war

by lancing sheep and cattle with their swords,
burning fields and crops. Anything to halt
Napoleon on his white horse, this last frenzied assault.

'*No. They don't like intruders,*' he said before his gaze
shifted its direction to settle on Catriona's face.

17

She imagined sometime that her unborn child might translate
Gaelic song into Cyrillic alphabet,

allowing melodies to be voiced alone or shared by choral
groups to sweep across the Baltic Sea or Urals,

providing warmth and cheer,
marking dates within the Gregorian year

celebrated, perhaps, by peasants, Alexandra, Nicholas
within the Imperial Ballroom of their Winter Palace,

each note laying roots deep within that distant soil.
'Thig crioch air an t-saoghal, ach mairidh gaol is ceol.'

18

The double-headed eagle.
Soiled portrait of Tsar Nicholas upon the cabin wall.
Bronze Horseman on the Thunder Stone.
A gaudy clutch of Matryoshka dolls.

It was these figures who stayed with her.
The knitted dresses. Coloured shawls.
Especially the hour that vessel sailed
from Skigersta quay with its curing bothy walls,

grief stirring within her,
aware that she was in his thrall
and her life starting to resemble
the host of Matryoshka dolls.

19

'I'll be back next season,'
she recalled Peadair say.
'No storm will provide cause or reason
for me to stay away.'

She held onto that promise every night
her parents watched her swollen body in dismay.

'I'll be back next season,'
but no one ever could have known
the winds that shook the seas that year
were like none that had ever blown,
men fastening the collars of their uniforms
before they set out in the storm.

'I'll be back next season,'
would be heard, too, on the mouths
of men from that part of the island
who left their family and house
to step into the fury of the tempest
that stormed both north and south.

'I'll be back next season,'
words that were often spoken
but for all the promise was sincere,
in these years it was all too often broken.

20

She heard no more about him.
Decades slowly turning,
Only the hammer
and sickle on a classroom wall
a reminder of his coming.

The face of Lenin, Stalin.
That nation's change of name
all distancing him from these shores.
She kept quiet, denied the claim

a Russian had fathered her son,
turned her head when others spoke of fish like ling
and how these men had strolled around the village.
Still, sometimes she heard voices sing

of the Volga boatmen,
'Heave ho! Heave ho! Once again, once more,'
the Gaelic song, too, about a fisherman
these nights she walked along the shore.

'Fhir a bhàta, na horo eile.
Fhir a bhàta, na horo eile.
Fhir a bhàta, na horo eile
Mo shoraidh slàn leat 's gach àit' an teid thu.'

'O boatman, nobody else.
O boatman, nobody else.
O boatman, nobody else.
My farewell to you, no matter where you go.'

SPUTNIK

Hector spent a week or two looking at Sheba's pups, sizing them up, giving them names, wondering which one he would choose. There was Snowy, for instance, white apart from a black dot at the tip of his tail. There was Sooty. She looked the complete opposite of her brother, black apart from a white blaze on her chest and a white flash at the end of her tail. And then there were the other two—the ones he had called Sputnik and Laika. With patches of white and black all over, they looked not unlike their mother. Lying on a rug in her corner of the barn, they scrambled blindly for her teats, four hungry mouths searching desperately for comfort and sustenance.

He had called them Sputnik and Laika for one reason.

'It's amazing,' his Dad had declared a fortnight earlier, shushing him as he listened to the wireless that November morning. 'The Russians have just put a dog into space.'

'Where? How? Why?' Words charged to his lips.

Dad didn't answer right away. He waited till the newsreader began talking about something called a Balance of Payments Crisis before he started. 'It's a dog called Laika. They put it in this rocket called Sputnik, sending it up into space to see if anything can live there.'

'And can it?'

'They seem to think it can. Anyway, it only said the animal's orbiting the earth. Going round and round in circles.'

'Wow! That's fantastic! What kind of dog is it?'

'It's probably a collie like Sheba. Black and white and good at chasing sheep. Or even a cow jumping over the moon.' He laughed at his own joke. 'Och, I can't remember, Hector. No doubt it'll tell you all about it in the papers tomorrow. You can read about it there.'

'Great,' he grinned. 'I'll do that.'

And for the next few days he scoured the papers for the first time in his life, reading all about the dog the Soviets had sent up into the stars. His name was the Russian word for 'Barker' and he was meant to be a little mongrel they had found in the streets of Moscow, a mix between a terrier and a husky. He clipped pictures of the animal from the *Express* and their next door neighbour's *Daily Record*; discovered that countries like Romania, Bulgaria and the USSR were all releasing stamps with the dog's head, all bright and alert, peering out at the surface of the moon; talked about it endlessly. He even learned a song about the animal. Mouthing the words of a Jamaican calypso singer called Mighty Sparrow , he danced around the kitchen, repeating—what he thought were the words of—its chorus:

'All these Sputniks sparkling in the night
Makes me sorry for the tiny dog in the Russian satellite ... '

Eventually, inevitably, his mother grew irritated by his endless lisping.

'Why don't you sing something else?' she'd complain, 'Some Gaelic song. 'Brochan Lom', perhaps. 'Balaich an

Iasgaich'. Or maybe that one about a dog you learned in school. The song about Pilot.'

'Oh, no, Mam,' he shuddered, thinking about that last song—a sad one about a dog that had lost its eye. That animal had just been called Pilot. Laika was more like a real one. His two eyes tracked the stars, looking out at the Milky Way, Orion, the Pole Star while he sat in the cockpit of his own space-rocket. 'The English one's far better.'

It was, though, the arrival of the pups a short time afterwards that kept Laika in Hector's mind. He watched Sheba waddle into the kitchen one morning. A change seemed to have come over her. She walked more slowly than usual, the darkness of her nipples apparent underneath her white undercoat.

'She's expecting puppies,' Mam had told him.

And then when they arrived, he asked a thousand questions.

'When do they learn to see?'

'Who's their Daddy?'

'Could they learn to fly?'

It was this last question that shocked Mam into silence.

'Could they what … ?'

'Like Laika. You know … ?' He sang a few lines from his calypso song again. *All these Sputniks sparkling in the night makes me sorry for the tiny dog …* Could they ever get the chance to fly?'

She laughed at him, ruffling his hair. 'Nach tu a' tha gorach, ille,' she grinned, commenting on how daft she thought he was. 'Of course not.'

Yet she didn't convince him. A few mornings later, he found Sheba away from the pups for the first time since their birth. Snow was on the way and Dad had brought the collie with him to drive his sheep up from the foot of the croft to the nearest field to the house. He had gone into the barn to find the pups unprotected, squealing and searching for their mother in the straw. Hector picked Sputnik up in his fingers. He squirmed and wrestled in his hand, a little black and white pup with short, smooth hair, a dark eyepatch over one eye. Kicking out his legs, he whimpered as the floor was taken from him, his small dark eyes staring in his direction.

'Sputnik, you have the honour to be chosen as pilot of this ship,' he declared.

Trembling, he took him up the ladder to the hayloft at the far end of the barn. He sat there in the darkness for a while, chatting to the dog, trying to soothe him.

'Shhh ... Shhh ... Keep quiet. It's all right. It's all right.'

He threw a few armfuls of hay down on the floor, trying to make sure Sputnik had a safe landing. It lay strewn there—a safety net for the sudden end of the pup's flight, if he failed to take off. He would put it back before Dad arrived home, certain that he would hear Sheba barking as she chased the sheep into the nearest field.

It was then he began to pitch the pup back and forth, swinging him, out into the darkness of the barn.

'Ten ... Nine ... Eight ...'

The pup whimpered again. He interrupted his countdown to try and soothe him.

'Four … Three … Two … One …'

The speed of his movement intensified.

'Blast off!'

He let him go—only to groan in disappointment as Sputnik failed to take flight. Take off failed to occur. He seemed to stay upright only for a short time before he dropped straight and suddenly to the ground, landing safely in the pile of straw. Racing down the ladder, he picked up the pup once again, deciding to repeat the exercise.

Sputnik would take flight.

He was sure of that.

Sputnik would take flight.

It was his Dad's arrival back at the house that saved Sputnik.

Hector heard his voice in the next field just after he had tried to send the pup into flight for the third time. He was shouting on Sheba to keep the flock together, making sure the animal was under control.

' Thig ann an seo! Come here!'

'Gu chois! Heel! … Aw, daing it! Nach eist thu rium. Gu chois! Heel!'

He rushed down the ladder to place Sputnik along with the other pups.

'It's okay,' he announced breathlessly, 'It's okay.'

He was still crouched above them, trying to reassure the pup when his Dad and Sheba entered the barn.

The collie raced towards her pups, licking and sniffing them, her tail wagging furiously as her offspring yelped around her.

'You been looking at them?' Dad said, patting Hector's head with a calloused hand.

'Aye … They're lovely.' Hector answered, aware of the smells his father often carried around with him. The sharp scent of mud and cow-dung on his boots. The greasy tang of sheep-wool on his fingers. 'I love playing with them.'

'Well, be careful of getting too attached to them.'

'Why?'

Dad shrugged his shoulders sadly. 'They won't be around here too much longer.'

Hector tried to argue with him. 'No … no,' he muttered, promising to look after them, care for them if they were allowed to stay on the croft.

'It's not possible,' Dad said sadly. 'There's only a place for Sheba at the moment.'

'You sure?'

'Sorry. Aye. I'm sure …'

He turned away then, leaving Hector to stare at the pups nuzzling their mother, seeking shelter in the warmth of her coat.

A few days later, they were gone.

Sheba whined and whimpered, barked once or twice, sniffing every inch of land around their crofthouse, trying her utmost to find her pups. In her distress, she even kept away from Hector, cowering when she saw him, looking up with deep and wounded eyes.

'What happened to them?' he asked.

Mam was the one he chose to question. She was in the kitchen at the time, preparing soup for his Dad's return home.

'We had to get rid of them, Hector. We don't need more than one.'

'We could have given them away.'

'Who to? People round here don't need a pup. Most have their own to look after.'

'But what did Dad do with them?'

She opened up the front of the stove, looking there for a moment to see if there was enough to keep their meal warm. After a moment, she sighed and stood up again, looking at him directly.

'He took them to the shore last night. He got rid of them there. Down at the geo.'

He knew where the geo was—a deep ravine where the waves had drilled through rock a short distance into the shoreline. It was where the villagers dumped much of their rubbish. The old, bird-pecked carcass of a sheep. A tangle of wire and fence-posts. Even on one occasion, an old car that had been mangled by crashing off the edge of the village road. Waves made short work of most of the debris, grinding and gnashing most of man's rust and refuse until it disappeared, sweeping it away below the depths of the ocean.

He could see his own Dad too, the way he had set out there. The pups would have been in the sack he carried in his hand. They sent out distress calls into the darkness, desperate to find their mother once again. Swinging forward and back, a heavy stone lying beside them, they were unaware where they were going, only conscious that this world was unfamiliar to them, these sounds, that smell—all becoming stranger as they made their way to the sea.

And then when he reached there, Dad would lift that sack high up in his fingers, swirling it round till it gathered force and speed, whirling it out towards the geo. It would toss and turn, spinning below stars and sky, sent out in the direction of the ocean, out below the Moon and Milky Way, the Pole Star, the Great Bear, the constellations that dotted and specked the giant arc of darkness that stretched above their heads. And in that infinite emptiness, he could see them become one with the real Laika and Sputnik, the satellite that circled and encompassed the earth, before they, too, burned cold and died, falling away towards the world's waters, snuffing out the light of life.

THE RED FLAG

'It waved above our infant might
When all ahead seemed dark as night ...'

1

I really can't remember but I bet
a name was etched upon a desktop
—a faintly pencilled requiescat,
'Murdo woz ere. October 62' —
and someone else had folded
a paper plane that flew
till it stalled and flopped
in a corner of the room.

And then we played some football
round the back
with Shonnie stuck in goals,
'Lev Yashin' kitted in the black
jumper he always wore
to school,
knitted from wool
remaining from the shawl
his Gran had worn since Iain's uncle
had been killed in the last war.

Back in class, we played with plasticine,
made boats
that never needed torpedoes
to prevent them staying afloat
while Alec drew huge, sprawling flames
he foresaw rising from the wood and tyres
piled to form the village bonfire
where out on edge of field and moor,
fireworks would be lit,
each rocket's whoosh,
each Roman candle's hiss and spit,
making fear and shadows flit
on the faces of our fathers
who'd all seen war before.

2

Shonnie always sought to be him.
That Black Cat, Lev Yashin.
He'd stop goals opponents might lash in
or prevent the ball from sailing over the wall.

Yet sail it often did. Sometimes it would land in
Nidsidh's turnips, potatoes, oats,
and we'd sneak over—as if we thought
we'd slipped through no-man's-land and into West Berlin,

scared that there might be searchlights on the wall
to trap us with their beams if we'd ever stumble, fall.

3

The night my anorak was draped
upon the washing-line,
a storm blew in to put it on.
Dad looked and said,
'It'll be in Siberia by dawn.'

Siberia. Snow like thistledown
blown round our croft.
Ice thick as sods of turf.
Cold sharp as nettles.
My fur-lined hood
would end up snared upon
a fur-lined wolf.
Or snagged upon the shoulders
of some Cold War Soviet soldier
preparing for the chill command
to drive the Cossacks' flocks of sheep
to graze upon our land.

Or so an old man told me—
the few acres of oats we'd sown
marked on invasion maps
for sickles to cut down.
Yet next day my anorak was found
ditched within a drain.
And my frozen Russian soldier
stamped his soles while waiting
for an order and an anorak
that never
ever
came.

4

In church that night they sprouted Astrakhans
and heavy coats fastened tight up to their throats
with fur collars and a wrap for frost-gnawed hands,
boots shielding toes against the onslaught
of a blizzard; more snow on layers that fell
the night before, whirling thickly till they kept
hearing in the sermon the tinkling of a troika's bells
sweeping across moorland, a wolf's sudden howls and yelps
casting its shiver through them, till they longed for home again,
the slip and slide of cars that would take them far
from here, to where their balalaikas played
and they could flex their fingers before the warmth of
    samovars.

5

They hailed the man hero of Crofting Labour
for all his work in increasing yields
of turnips, oats, potatoes in neat fields
that were the envy of both foes and neighbours.

Yet all his seed now practise the art
of ploughing reams of paper with their pens,
stacking grant forms, applications
while those around them marvel at the craft

in fences that surround barren ground,
acres scored by rabbit footprints,
the drill and click of printer's ink—
sole rhythms that their labours have laid down.

6

The moon was sometimes like that down in Barra.
A big and bright bodhran at night
with clouds that boomed and banged
upon its surface until a drum of dance began
and Seamus popped outdoors to step
into raindrops that helter-skeltered down,
washing clean his grease paint till
he lost his usual mask of gravity
and spiralled loose to reel and play the clown.

And he was such a wonder in the thunder.
A lightning jig performed in puddles
as feet kicked against the traces, pull
and tug of water while laughter cracked
canyons deep across his face
till its frenzied rhythm unhinged him
from Ardveenish, Bolnabodach,
the first Hebridean sputnik that skipped the light fantastic
and vamoosed into space.

7

Many have pondered how the Cossack dance
came first to these islands—
a shift that came about by historic chance
when Lochgelly's finest leather was wielded in the hand

of that headmaster MacMichael, whose skill was such
that he could split a matchstick with a quick
swish of his wrist. We all admired the fierceness of his touch,
especially the day he crashed it down on the palm and
     finger-tips

of Norman for the crime of tugging some girl's hair.
We recall the boy's frenzy—the folding of his arms,
the way his bare legs flailed the air,
the cry—in the Cyrillic alphabet—that showed us his alarm.

THE TALE OF A SHOE
After Gogol

There will be some who will say that this story does not stand up, that it is not sufficiently grounded in reality. They will claim this simply because I am the teller of the tale, arguing not only that I am an unreliable narrator but also an incredible one, a loose and flapping tongue utterly without conviction for the average reader. Let them argue this if they wish. I have been an unquiet spirit in these islands for too many years, suffered too many knocks and scuffs throughout my long existence for their objections to concern me overmuch.

I am a shoe. Not a modern, stylish item of footwear fashioned to show off to advantage a woman's slim and well-turned ankle. Nor one designed to protect and cherish a well-known footballer's metatarsal bone. Instead, I am one of these basic foot-guards your ancestors might have called a 'tackety boot', consisting mainly of stiff, black leather, flaps and tongue, fine stitching, stout heel and sole armoured by studs, a series of metal eyelets that once allowed thick dark laces to weave in and out, culminating in the tightest of knots. However, even the right and privilege of bearing a foot has long been denied to me. For the best part of a century, I have lain where I am today— mouldering deep within moorland peat, waiting for one of the local crofters to release me from the dampness of its clutch as he sets out to obtain fuel for his winter fires.

And when he does this, he will expose more than me. He will also reveal the truth of my story; the bare bones of all that happened over seventy years ago no longer hidden but once again on view. It is at this time my tongue will be listened to once again; people will wonder what my eyelets might have witnessed; and those who doubt my words will finally have to admit that my feet have remained firmly rooted on (or is it in?) this earth ...

When I was younger, there was no question where I belonged.

For the best part of a year, I was a permanent fixture on someone's foot—that of Archie Mackay, the local minister's son. He wore me and my long decayed companion, the right shoe, all his active hours. My sole brushed and touched many different surfaces during these months. Heather—when Archie leaped over moorland ditches. Grass—when he made his way across the machair. Sand—when he traipsed nearby beaches. Cow-dung—as he stepped carelessly over fields where cattle grazed.

And I felt honoured to protect him in all these places. Pleased that I had been chosen to fit a youthful foot. Glad to obtain the privilege of preventing cuts and bruises, the chaffing of his toes. Proud, especially, that this task had been granted me when winter was on its way, its winds set to chill a young boy's every nerve and bone.

Yet for all that, I felt, too, a sense of unease. Partly this was caused by the size and stature of the child I had been assigned to guard. A plump, unfit boy, he panted and puffed every time he ran, creating a great deal of worry and concern for those whose role in life was to keep him upright. Partly, too, my misgivings were created by the fact that Archie was not the most pleasant-natured of children, possessing a whole series of characteristics that shoes have always tended to dislike.

There was his inattentiveness. Whenever anybody would talk about God and religion, his feet would become restless, heels clicking as he sat in a church pew. He would do this even when his father told interesting stories from the Bible—the tale of Samson and Delilah or David grounding the huge figure of Goliath with a slingshot and a stone. While others would listen carefully to the voice explaining, 'David prevailed over the Philistine with a sling and with a stone and smote the Philistine, and slew him,' his response would be to lean back in his chair, swinging the weight of his feet to and fro.

What concerned me most, however, was the way that the majority of Archie's unappealing characteristics were connected with my presence on his feet. He was loud and boastful about the fact that he was the owner of a decent pair of brogues, sparking his studs, for instance, on an edge of rock.

'Look at me!' he would shout, 'I could start a fire with these. Bet you couldn't do the like of that.'

Or else there would be the times when he would run helter-skelter towards a pond, splashing his companions with mud and dirt.

'You should see your faces!' he would laugh.

There was no chance of others his age even attempting such tricks. The village boys—Seumas, Alec, Angus John—went barefoot round the village; their parents unable to afford even the most basic type of footwear to protect their feet. They spent their time glowering at both me and my companion, envious of the fact that their parents were unable to provide such well-shod items for their toes.

And I had sympathy for them. For, if there is one thing that a shoe learns during an existence that is often nasty, brutish and short, it is compassion for the human foot. I must confess to having experienced that emotion many times when I glanced over in the direction of Seumas, Alec and Angus John that winter. Little – either literally or metaphorically – guarded them against the knocks and bruises of life, while my owner displayed his advantages so blatantly that they could not help but feel resentment towards him. Whether he was aware of it or not, his every word and step left its imprint on their feelings.

Take his football, for instance. He was the only one in the village who owned such an item, obtaining one for his birthday—in itself an alien idea for the rest of his schoolmates. He would take it each day to school or their makeshift pitch on the machair, ostensibly to allow the others to take part in a game.

In practice, though, this did not prove to be the case. As well as owning the ball, Archie commanded it. When it was in play, he made sure that no one else had any say in its movements, snatching it off the field if things were not rolling his way.

'It's a foul! ... I tell you it's a foul! If you don't agree with me, I'll tell you exactly what I'll do. I'll go home right now and take the ball with me. Immediately. Straight away. Now.'

There were other problems. Despite the fact Archie wore shoes upon his feet, protecting him from the impact of ball, stones and tackles, he was worse than a beginner at the sport. The rest of the boys were better than him – sprites dancing round a giant's feet – taking the ball away, defeating him easily, only to hear an inevitable chorus of complaint when he was defeated.

'It's not a goal! … I tell you it isn't! If you lot don't listen, I'll tell you exactly what I'll do. I'll go home right now and take the ball with me. Immediately. Straight away. Now.'

It was this display of bad grace that led to the rock being thrown. Archie stalked off the field with the ball under his arm, engaged in one of his customary tantrums. Without even thinking, Angus John bent down to pick up the stone, a fist-sized chunk of Lewisian gneiss, and threw it hard in Archie's direction. It whirled through the air, ending its flight in the middle of his forehead.

And then Goliath tumbled. My sole no longer fixed upon the earth, he toppled backwards, allowing me to see sky, grass and the drained faces of the other three boys as they raced towards Archie. I heard a groan from his mouth, felt a shudder passing through his body. I listened, too, to the voices of the boys as they panicked round my owner.

'Look at the bruise on his head.'

'His nose is bleeding …'

'His mouth is too …'

'Hell …'

'He's dead, isn't he?'

'What on earth are we going to do?'

It was Alec's older brother, Murdo, who provided the answer to that question. When he was brought from the field where he had been working a short distance away, he spoke calmly, sensibly, trying to help the youngsters.

'We can't tell the police … If we do, Angus John might hang for it. Or at least go to prison for years to come. His father will demand it. And you know what the judge will probably be like. Take his word for gospel just because he's a minister. And all because of a silly, stupid accident. It just wouldn't be right.'

And so it came about—the decision that brought to an end my familiarity with daylight. My time of stepping over soil was over; my years of rotting under it just beginning. Archie's body was taken on the back of Murdo's cart to a small stretch of moorland a few miles from his home. Turf was cut and lifted; peat sliced and dug out; a grave created for my owner. They heaved and hauled him into this, grateful for a small heather-covered mound that lay between them and the public road, protecting their actions from view. And then they covered him up, pressing firmly down and flattening the disturbance they had made on the surface of the moor. While they were doing this, Angus John was sobbing, filled with remorse over what he had done.

'It was all an accident. Honest. All an accident.'

While all this was going on, however, I was most concerned with my own personal vanity. I hoped that both my companion and I would be removed from Archie's feet, to fit, perhaps, those of one of the young men who had buried him, to allow me to walk once more over green and fertile land, to leap over pools and streams, to wade through water. There is nothing a shoe likes less than to see its usefulness come to an end long before it becomes battered and misshapen.

Or that I might even be discovered after Archie's father raised a hue and cry, urging the police to discover where his son might have gone. If he did do this, however, he was only met with silence and denial from the villagers, anxious to protect their own rather than see a town-dweller's idea of justice being done. The old men shrugged their shoulders. Women pursed their lips. The boys with whom he had been playing football claimed they had seen him head off home some time before. Perhaps he had gone in the direction of the sea. Or the moor. The young lad had a nasty habit of wandering off on his own sometimes.

Meantime, I just lie here—mouldering and decaying. Sometimes I brood about the condition of my partner. It slipped off while Archie was tossed into his makeshift grave and looks down on me in a bashed and broken state, its loose and flapping sole grinning maniacally in my direction. And I long to escape its gaze. To sprout, perhaps, a small set of wings on each side. To stretch them and rise from this ground where I have lain for far too long. To put an end to the sense of injustice I have nursed for over seventy years. To become a small part of one of these angels Archie's father was always on about, looking downwards from a cloud in the heavens instead of being cloaked for an eternity in the damp and dark of peat …

CAPONE AND DOSTOEVSKY

Hypocrisy is a dying art in these islands. Every weekend, there's a queue buying scratchcards and DVDs at the local shop. 'Give me those lucky dips, Martin,' they announce to the shopkeeper. Or, 'I'll take this film. And that one,' they say, placing the empty cases on the counter. 'I need something to pass the time on a Sunday afternoon.'

Duncan Macdonald – the church elder that some twenty years ago we all knew better as Capone – would have stood for none of that. A tall powerful figure in his grey overcoat and hat, his eyes had the sharpness of a gannet's gaze. For all that he was in his seventies, one look would have been enough to terrify the likes of Martin, his hand sweeping over these goods like Jesus chastising the moneychangers in the temple. 'What do you mean selling stuff like that? It may do a lot for your profits, but it won't do much for your soul!' And then his glare would swirl round his fellow-shoppers. 'Gambling! Breaking the Sabbath! What do you mean by doing such things?'

One time I was on the wrong side of this look was a few short weeks before he died. A young student, I was reading *Crime and Punishment* near the back of a crowded bus when he came to sit beside me.

'What's that you've got there?'

I told him.

'Now tell me … Do you ever spend time reading the Bible? I bet you never spend much time doing the likes of that.'

I smiled weakly in response. There are some people with whom it is a waste of breath to quarrel.

Yet in his youth, Capone never spent much time studying the Bible. If rumours are to be believed, he was never still long enough to lift the Good Book. Instead, he would be scaling rocks on the shoreline; balancing on one leg or combing his hair while standing on a stone outcrop that jutted out a hundred feet over the ocean and daring others to follow his example.

'I bet you couldn't do that.'

He would clamber on the roofs of the village blackhouses too, blocking the chimney with a large flat stone or a piece of turf or wood. As the inhabitants ran from their smoke-choked home, he would be hiding behind a nearby wall, trying to choke down his own laughter.

'I bet they don't know what's happened to them.'

'I bet ...' Even in his years as a church elder, this phrase would be like a nervous tic on his lips. 'I bet you don't think often of your salvation ... I bet you don't read the Bible like you should ...' In the years before he found the Church, however, these words were more than habit. They clicked continually on his tongue as he played cards and dice with the men with whom he worked on the Hydro schemes in places like Cannich, Cluanie and Glencarn. Phrases like 'I bet', 'I raise', 'Ace of Hearts', and 'Jack of Diamonds' formed part of the only common language of their camps.

People from the battered ends and edges of all over Europe learned to use it. There were Highlanders and islanders; poor Irish from the ragged coastline of Donegal—coming from communities where steady work was rare and intending to return when things had changed. And then there were those known as the 'Poles' – the displaced men of not only Poland but also countries the others never knew existed – like Lithuania, Ukraine, Estonia. Unlike the West Coasters and Irish, they had been forced to surrender many of their dreams of return. Looking over their shoulders at nations lost either to bloodshed or tyranny, they had little choice but to try and begin new lives on the strange and alien landscape they had chanced upon.

For all their differences, the groups had much in common. In slow and faltering English, they could each tell stories about the frailty and precariousness of life. Poverty and weakness had helped to make them that way; the sound of money in their pockets – crisp notes and coins – a more comforting rhythm than the pulse of their hearts. Only a good wage in their hands could grant them a short spell of security, a time of calm and ease.

The author Capone caught me reading, Fyodor Dostoevsky, would have known much better than me how they felt. Never from a rich family, his father, murdered by serfs, left little for his widow and children. This turned the young Fyodor into a radical—so much so that he was imprisoned for political reasons by Tsar Nicholas I. He made, too, an early, disastrous marriage to a widow who suffered from consumption and had a son from her first husband. He was also involved with a magazine banned by the Russian government. A short time later, his wife and brother died. At one stage, he even had to pawn his clothes for food.

And throughout all this, there was gambling. The gaming tables at Weisbauden in Germany. The spinning roulette wheel. Roll of dice. Cut of cards. Eyes shut and hoping for a glimpse of luck. A change of life. It was the same with the men in the hydro camp. The boredom of isolation. Stench of sweat and grime. The prospect of poverty when this spell of work came to an end. All this made them gather nightly at a table in the centre of their hut; the words 'I bet …', 'flush', 'pontoon', 'I raise …' never requiring any translation for this multi-national group of men whose blackened fingers stained the cards within their hands. As they coughed up the dust of earth and boulder that had gathered in their lungs, the pile of coins gleamed brightly. To have it in their fingers meant the oblivion of whisky. Or another kind of oblivion—a new life that would help them escape the horrors of the old.

Capone never knew good luck.

His friend and fellow villager, Murdo Dan, would remind him of this every time he rose from these late-night sessions with his pockets empty. The young fair-headed man with his round, red face scabrous with spots would chide him with a look. And then, as a believer, he would try to comfort him by saying:

'You're not one of those blessed by the devil. I think instead you've been chosen by the Lord.'

Capone would react in much the same way as others did to his own remarks some fifty years later—snorting with derision at Murdo Dan's display of faith. He was thinking of other ways of gambling, trying his luck as a 'Tunnel Tiger' – one of the men who blasted through rock to help create the dam – instead of earning a smaller wage as a labourer.

'I'm going to volunteer to be one,' he told Murdo Dan one morning.

'You sure?'

'Aye ... I need the money. I've lost too much lately.'

Murdo Dan stared at him. It was usually the 'Poles' or the Irish who volunteered for this job. Ready to risk all for a little cash, they would burrow in tunnels undercutting rock, placing sticks of explosives – like pink candles – into holes drilled in the stone. Sometimes things would go amiss. They would go too deep and the section above them would collapse, drowning them in mud and clay. Or something might go wrong with the gelignite, blasting caps and timer they had in their possession and a blast would make the hills and trees tremble. Blood, flesh and bone would mingle with boulders sliding loose. Dark stone tinged with red tumbling down a mountainside.

'You can't be thinking of doing that. You're mad.'

Capone shrugged. 'Sometimes you have to be.'

But then – an hour or so later – proof came of madness. A sign that shook all these men swinging their pickaxes through fissures in the stone or shovelling clay.

The lorry-drivers, too, transporting their loads through the narrow roads of the Highlands. They heard the blast as it echoed through the vastness of that glen, ending like a given note. They caught the tang of acrid smoke as it hung in the air. It was followed by whispers, voices that told of a young 'Pole' – Jan Ilvolglin – killed in an accident. Splinters of his skin and bone would be encased and coffined in the cement and stone of the Glencarn Dam, the shards of his body indistinguishable from shards of rock. Murdo Dan's head bowed for a moment before turning once more to his fellow-villager.

'You won't do it. Will you?'

Capone trembled—the audacity of his gamble suddenly becoming clear. 'No. I won't.'

'You promise?'

'Aye.'

'Good,' Murdo Dan grinned as he began digging once again, his shovel cutting into the clay.

But he couldn't resist another remark—one delivered a few paces away from Capone's side.

'Doesn't what happened prove anything to you? It's as I always said. The Lord thinks of you as one of His own.'

Dostoevsky would have understood a mind like Murdo Dan's—his life transformed into a sequence of signs and symbols, moments when the salvation and grace of God became clear.

In his twenties, as part of a radical group, Fyodor had been arrested—the frozen hush and quiet of a

Russian winter ended by the thunder of army boots and rifles breaking into his home. They had taken him to Semyonsky Square in the centre of St Petersburg, lining him up with others against the wall of one of its largest buildings. He stood there, shivering in the light summer clothes in which he had been arrested, snow swirling around him, frost gnawing into his skin. His eyes shut as he waited for the soldiers' fingers to tighten around the triggers of their rifles.

But the bullet never came. At the last moment, Tsar Nicholas I ordered a reprieve, arriving just a few moments before the guns were set to fire. Instead, the prisoners were sent to Siberia where Dostoevsky spent the following four years. On their long march, they stopped at the town of Tobolsk where a group of old peasant women greeted them, giving the prisoners a bundle of goods—some tea, candles, cigars, a copy of the New Testament with ten roubles sown in its binding.

That single act of goodness transformed Dostoevsky. Abandoning his radical friends and ideas, he turned instead to Christ and the Orthodox Church. In his works – *Crime and Punishment, The Possessed, The Brothers Karamazov* – he rails against those who have surrendered Russian faith and traditions for what he perceived as the faithless and empty life of the West, asking the same questions as Capone might do today.

'Do you abandon God and your own traditions for these trivialities, these worthless toys?'

*

Yet for much of his time in the camp, Capone eluded the hold of the faith he later criticised others for abandoning. Murdo Dan would try again and again to trap his soul during his times away from the gambling table, while they were dressing in the morning or working together on the dam.

'Don't you think it's time you listened to your conscience?'

The moment came, however, when the twenty-four year old least expected. A roll of notes and stack of coins lay beside him on the table. Cards were splayed between his fingers. The Kings of Hearts, Spades, Diamonds. Three, four, five and six of Clubs. He grinned contentedly.

'Rummy.'

He reached for the money. As he did so, a young Pole – Josef Gilius – clutched his outstretched hand. Capone looked up to see a wolflike grin on the man's face, his blue eyes icy with anger.

'No, Jock … You cheat.'

'I didn't.'

'You bloody well did.'

An instant later, the Pole came on him, closing around his neck, all hair and hot breath, bristling skin and sharp fingers. His wolf-sharp teeth clamped on his ear, biting hard into him. Capone pushed him away, the table and chairs crashing down in their struggle.

'Bloody cheat! … Thief!'

The Pole launched himself at Capone again, dodging the labourers who tried to restrain him. His blue shirt was black with earth and grease; blood in the scrapes and scratches on his skin. Capone's hands rose to squabble with him, forcing him away as he was swung from side to side. His attacker's teeth were bared as he screamed in accusation.

'You have stolen my money, you filthy, stinking Jock!'

And then a sharp pain stabbed through the islander, as a filed-down cut-throat razor swung in an arc towards his chest. He dropped to the floor where a few moments later, his fellow-workers gathered, propping him up while others held back the enraged Pole. Blood seeped through his vest and shirt. He felt as if he had eaten something evil and harmful and he tried to spit it out – blood, sickness and saliva – spitting again and again. In the clamour of the room, he heard one voice speaking calmly and quietly, and recognised it to be that of Murdo Dan.

'We have to staunch the wound. Otherwise, we'll lose him.'

It was Murdo Dan who saved him.

He sat beside him in the front of the lorry that took him to the hospital. Capone could only half-remember their slow progress along the road that twisted its way across the breadth of the Highlands towards Inverness, barely able to see in the sliver of new moon he could occasionally glimpse above the mountains or see reflected in the waters of a loch. Above the noise of the lorry engine, he could sometimes hear Murdo Dan talking, indulging in a litany of village gossip or a moment of prayer.

'Oh Lord, spare this man—one I have known since childhood. I recognise that he is not without fault …'

He saw him once again in the hospital. In his moments free from delirium, he would look up to see Murdo Dan—his face with its usual plague of spots. The man would smile cheerfully. Capone would hear his voice fade in and out of range.

'The doctors say you're a very lucky man. An inch further down and he'd have got you in the heart. Isn't that proof?'

And then the moment came when that face was no longer present. Capone stared round his empty sideward, searching for the presence of his friend. There was no sign of him, but instead, his hand brushed against a large envelope lying on the blankets. As he opened it , much of its contents slipped from his fingers. A pack of Capstan dropping to the floor. The money he had won at the gambling table showering across the ward. But one thing remained tight within his grip—the copy of the Bible Murdo Dan had left behind for him.

Capone took it as a sign.

He'd talk about his days in the hydro camp at church-meetings or at the fireside of an island home, telling about how he had dodged and avoided God's providence until that moment of revelation and release. 'I was never lonely after that day in the hospital,' he would say. 'Never that long ill either. The doctors told me I made a remarkable recovery. Brand new in a few short weeks.'

He would pause for a moment before turning his gaze on the congregation, working up to a punchline he had used a thousand times before.

'And I bet all these doctors thought their hard work and medicine had cured me. But I knew much better than that. Instead, I put my life down – whole and complete – on a racing certainty. A sure-fire thing. Not on wealth or riches.' His gaze would swirl accusingly over the fine hats worn by several women in the church. 'Not on alcohol.' Another hard and intense look, this time on the local bachelors. 'Not on any of the words of men.' His gaze switched in my direction. 'But on the word of God. The only true and sure bet a man can place in this world.'

Yet even that didn't seem so certain in the hours before he died.

That happened one of these wild and stormy nights that so often afflict this edge of the world. The rain was like a hammer pounding windows and roof; the wind sharp on flesh and bone. Fences leaned before the weather's power. Sheep sheltered. Even the electricity that Capone and the others had worked hard to supply switched on and off for an hour or so before, finally, giving up completely. Capone turned up at his neighbour Matilda Morrison's house with a torch in hand, face chilled and white.

'Could you give the doctor a ring for me? I'm no' feeling so good.'

In the hours that followed, a new pain seared his chest. The nurse and doctor who came to his home heard him curse and swear, using words that had not been on his lips for decades.

'The Ace and Queen of Spades. That's how the cards have been cut for me. Isn't it, Doctor? Isn't it?'

He experienced, too, the same sort of delirium as the one Dostoevsky imagined Raskolnikov going through in the closing pages of *Crime and Punishment*, or which the author himself might have suffered in one of the epileptic seizures that so often affected him. His shouting echoed through the ambulance taking him to the hospital in Maransay.

'The mountains! They're bloody falling. There's a lad in there. Trapped in the tunnel. Will no-one round here do anything to save him? Will no-one round here do bloody anything?'

And then, there were the ambulance-men holding him down, wrestling with all the power, anger and hate that remained in his body till they manage to roll open his shirtsleeve, injecting the needle into his arm, death clouding his vision as he fell asleep.

AND QUIET FLOWS THE DONALD...

And quiet flows the river
I once strolled beside in Dell.

Past walls where they once (illegally) distilled
whisky; where they filled

barrows with peats they wheeled
across tracks and turf; where men often sat to tell

stories of their childhood, of how the watermill
used to grind oats and barley till

history turned its quern-stones silent, still;
where crofters used to carry buckets to the nearest well;

the currents where our football
often splashed and fell.

Or the hike down to the beach where waves swirled
continually; where neighbours stood within the shade
    of cliff and hill

and thought of their lost kin in America,
that they would meet again one day

if all their dreams and visions were fulfilled.

'POLISH' SONGS OVERHEARD
AT THE HYDRO DAM

Not of Peigi Bhàn nor Roisin Dhubh nor any girl they
    loved
nor of boats to Carrickfergus, Skye or home to
    Ballyjamesduff
but the wads within their wallets when they were at
    last paid off.

Not of Uig's beaches nor of Gweedore's sands
nor the chant of prayer or rosary nor the swell and fall
    of psalms
but the knowledge there was more than muck that still
    clung to their hands.

Not the embrace of a mother nor a father's restrained smile
nor the neighbour's cheerful question—*'Are you with
    us for a while?'*
but the coldness of that pale sun witnessed in exile.

Not of heather, shamrock nor of need for the Auld Sod
nor the faith in Jesus lost in Highland rain and fog
but the thought of fields they once ploughed, fertilised
    by their friends' blood,

And that agony of absence for which glass brings no relief,
the knowledge that your homeland has been stolen, seized,
the bones of lost relations, the grime and grit and grief.

OUTLINE FOR A FILM SCRIPT
IN THE LONG TRADITION OF
SOVIET SOCIALIST REALISM

Figures from that epic used to reel
out in endless orbit round our moor.
Boy meets tractor; falls in love,
rolled off his feet by giant wheels;
power of clutch and engine,
till exhausted by her energy,
his world swings on its axle
and he turns his headlights in a new direction.

Yet that track never cuts too deep.
His love of cars, wine, women,
barely skims the surface
and the thought of past affection keeps
accelerating pulse and nerve until
his love for his sweet Massey's finally restored;
foot back upon her pedal,
hand tight upon the smooth curve of her wheel.

THE DEATH OF TOLSTOY

At 8 am, old Tolstoy came to call
on the staff working at the ferry terminal,
though rain drummed upon the carpark and storm and
     ocean squalled.
'I've come to see the ferryman,' he said.

Patiently we told him there would be long delays,
that a hurricane was stirring and would hold us in its sway
tonight and tomorrow. *'It will blow for several days.'*
'I've come to see the ferryman,' he said.

At ten o'clock, it was clear he was waiting yet,
sitting in his plastic chair, tired and short of breath.
His skin was ghoulish; eyelids shut; features soaked
     with sweat.
'I've come to see the ferryman,' he said.

At noon his wife and child appeared, thrashed by wind
     and rain.
We watched them sit beside him, endeavour to explain
that he'd lost himself these last few days, mind besieged
     by pain.
'I've come to see the ferryman,' he said.

By two, we heard the whispers; a woman who'd been left
hungry by this man squandering his wealth,
both bank account and furniture cleared away in stealth.
'I've come to see the ferryman,' he said.

Two hours later and the neighbours came to whisper
over his head
a gale of tales and rumours that hushed the stilling of
his breath.
They were about to lift him from his chair when they
noticed he was dead.
'He's gone to see the ferryman,' one of the people said.

SONG FOR A TSAR

(I.M. Catherine Mackinnon, born Uisken,
Isle of Mull, c. 1778. Children's nurse to the
household of Alexander I. Died Florence, Italy,
1858. Buried – allegedly – St Petersburg,
Russia, 1859)

1

Winter's Palace, St Petersburg. The moon is full
as Catherine seeks to calm and lull
the child to sleep with verse and music learned long
   ago in Mull.

Both years and miles have swelled
since then, but she is conscious that the roll
and pitch of tides are in that song—for all that different
   squalls

may stir and rock his life, its rhythms will come back
to wrap around him, these moments he wears mourning
   black,
that instant he is startled by the crack

of gunshot, those hours when weight of robe and crown
bestowed upon him will bend both neck and head down.
He'll recall then that song with which she gifted him,

and all the flow and cadence of its foreign sounds.

2

Sometimes she would smell the reek of peat
and think: This is where I come from,
these houses where blown ash sweeps
earthen floors like snow stacked deep
upon the tundra, where hunger keeps
stalking souls whose only sustenance is prayer,

and she'd note the presence of a hush
rarely in attendance when tides crushed
the beach at Uisken; the only sounds
the distant howling of a wolf,
the crackling of ice and frost
taking solid grip of ground and air,

and she missed the meagre meals,
richness of song her people shared.

3

The bright lights of a chandelier
could not hold a candle's gleam
to *fir chlis* or foxfire
which she on winter's nights had seen

pirouetting above Moscow,
waltzing over the Ross of Mull,
its splendour putting in the shade
the Romanovs and nobles at those balls

swirling round the Kremlin,
with Princes in pressed uniforms, Princesses in gowns,
each one only a thin shadow
of the aurora's dazzling crown.

4

Florence, 1858. A sudden chill
afflicts Catherine, as she is conscious that there will
come a day when Uisken is empty, still,

cleared of homes and people. And that child whose cries
were soothed and quietened by that lullaby
learned long ago in Mull will lie

near the canal that bears her forename, his body enmeshed
in snow and tattered greatcoats, broken swords, ripped
        epaulettes,
entrails of both guard and emperor, torn confusion of
        the flesh.

5

But before then, the song on Alexander's tongue
granted him by Catherine while he wept when young
resounds across both stone and iron-fisted ground
where they lay this stranger down.

'Nuair thèid mac mo righ-sa
fo làn èideadh
gu robh neart na cruinne leat
's neart na grèine
neart an tairbh dhuibh
's àirde leumas ...'

When the son of my king
steps out in full robes,
may he have strength of the globe
and force of shining sun,
the power of the dark bull
that leaps most high ...

Those Gaelic words are left
to travel across taiga and the steppes
and wash up near Fionnphort, Bunessan,
the cleared townships of the Ross of Mull
to tell the few natives who remain there
that this exile's heart is quiet and still.

I DREAM OF MIKHAIL GORBACHEV
*(An Extract from Russian Government Files
Discovered 9/10/2007)*

16 Cairnbost
Isle of Raws
6th October 1999

My Dear Mikhail,

I am writing to you because I am alone and I know you are too. The kids have left home now and Andy's in his usual place, sitting in the corner of the Smithy Bar with a nip and a half-pint in front of him. No doubt he'll be mumbling too about how he'd do anything for his country and how the English are always keeping him and the rest of us Scots down. It's not that I've ever noticed him clambering to his feet to do anything about it. After all, as my father used to say, it's far easier for the likes of Andy to moan about how someone else is glueing his bum to his seat than shoving a thistle down the back of his breeks to get him off it.

Anyway, I shouldn't complain. You're alone for different, sadder reasons. Your wife Raisa's gone now, taken from your side by cancer, and today and for the rest of your life, you face the prospect of living your days without her. I feel for you, my dear, sweet Mikhail with your dark eyes touched by sadness, that crimson mark always on your face, when I think of how lonely it must be for you now. There is no doubt she was bright and beautiful, a remarkable woman of her or any other time. I can remember so many things about her – how she made the little children of Reykjavik laugh and smile at all her stories, driving Nancy Reagan mad with jealousy at the way she charmed them all and what she said when she came to London that year – that she would rather visit Marks and Spencer than go to Karl Marx's grave. How you must have chuckled when she came out with things like that. How too she must have made the old comrades around you bristle and choke in fury, muttering about how unsuitable she was for a man in your position, a leader of the Communist Party, the one in charge of the entire Soviet Union. For all their complaints, there is no doubt that someone like that would have lightened your eyes and heart when shadows came to your family later in life. There was the time, for instance, when these nasty, brutish generals, all trying to bring the old ways and certainties back, imprisoned you inside your holiday home. There was the moment too when, for all your smartness and intelligence, you realised that power had been snatched from you by an old, drink-sodden clown.

There is a man in our community whom I know must feel like that. Every time I see his face at the front of the kirk, I think of you, Mikhail. Alasdair has the same sad eyes, balding head, even a red birthmark just like yours, though, in his case, it spreads along his right cheek. He wears the same grey hat and coat as you did too, a dark scarf around his neck. I watch him take these off every time he goes to kirk—hanging the coat and scarf in the vestibule, placing his hat on a peg—and I remember the days he used to come to our house when he was younger and turned his eyes shyly in my direction, his mouth becoming dry of words each time he looked at me.

It was my father he spoke to most. He'd talk to him about hiring out his tractor and the money he made hauling peats home for this or that one. He had a digger, too, and he'd sit in it for hours on end, scooping a ditch out of some boggy, waterlogged stretch of land or digging the foundations for a home.

'Steady as he goes, Mr Morrison. Steady as he goes. That's what they always say about me. Steady as he goes.'

'You're Mr Perfection when you sit behind these controls.' Dad would nod and smile. 'You've got a great reputation in this place, Alasdair. There's no denying that.'

'Och, well,' he'd blush, 'It's like my own father always told me. You've got to guard your own name on this island. Make sure you look after it as carefully as you can. There's all too many ready to steal it from you. And once you do, you'll never get it back.'

'Aye. Aye.' Dad would turn away, raising his eyebrows and looking in my direction. There were times he'd pretend to stifle a mock-yawn when Alasdair was in his company. 'Mr Steady-and-Serious,' he called him behind his back. 'So slow he keeps stalling.'

He wasn't the only one who found him that way. The village girls weren't slow in letting me know how tedious they found my admirer to be.

'He's not here again, is he?' Mairi might ask.

'You fairly draw a good crop of Casanovas to this crofthouse, don't you, Elizabeth? How can you put up with the likes of him?'

Yet I now see he would have been fairly easy to put up with. I watch his hands these days as he puts his Bible before him on the pew. They're strong hands. Neat and clean. Nails trimmed and clipped. Skin scrubbed and unsullied by any of the dirt left behind after his work. There's a wholesome smell about him too. Soap and a tiny splash of after-shave. Imperial Leather. A bottle that must have been bought twenty years ago. Suit pressed. Shirt ironed. Shoes polished. There's not even a speck of dandruff on his shoulders.

And all that cleanliness is not just part of his appearance. It's also in the way he acts and talks and behaves. There is the consideration he displays when a woman enters the kirk alongside him. He opens the door, ushers her through, and all the time, he is speaking softly, graciously, talking that way to everyone he encounters in his daily business.

'Is there anything else you'd like me to do?' he says when he's finished his work. 'Remember to call me anytime you'd like.'

I imagine he's much like you in that way: the quiet, ready smile for others, the way you'd succeed in winning over even those with whom you disagreed, people like Ronald Reagan and Margaret Thatcher. (She even said the first time you met that you were a man with whom the West could do business.) And you know, for once, she was right. Here was a man with whom all mankind could do business. Someone on whom the whole world could build its trust.

I want to confess something to you, Mikhail. I turned down a man who could be relied on and trusted.

A Mr Steady-As-He-Goes. A gentleman with a sound reputation. He turned to me one evening after he had finished clearing out one or two of the drains on my father's croft. It was work he never charged for, hoping, perhaps, that his generosity might encourage someone like me to look at his sad, brown eyes with favour. When he had finished working, he sat in the kitchen, swallowing – as neatly and tidily as he always did – the tea and scones I had prepared for him.

'Elizabeth,' he said, 'Can I ask you something?'

'Yes?'

'Would you like to go on a date with me? Perhaps for a meal, eh? To the Imperial Hotel in town or some place else you might like? Or a dance or a concert sometime? Or even for a wee run somewhere to Marnwick perhaps or Sulishader?'

He may have said more. He had a tendency to ramble sometimes, allowing his words to race and blur together, digging a ditch for himself with his speech. But I barely heard him. Instead, I was picturing the mocking faces of my friends, the embarrassment I would feel if they ever heard of this request. *'What? The tractor-driver? What made him think he could ever reverse his way into your bed? You let him park too long on your sofa.'* I imagined a lifetime of small humiliations and embarrassments. The jokes and jibes they would all make at my expense.

I said no.

'You're sure?' he asked. 'You can take time and think it over.'

'I'm sure.'

They are words I have regretted coming out of my mouth a thousand times since, Mikhail, but all I saw that day before me was a man whose only pillow-talk would consist of a thousand tales about tractors, the size of their loads and engines, the tracks and trails he had successfully taken his giant wheels and trailers that day.

'You know what I did the first time I got that new tractor of mine? Took her right to the top of the beinn just to see what I could do with it, how I could push her to the limit.'

(I've just had a thought, Mikhail. You must be familiar with men like Alasdair. You probably came across quite a few in the time you were Governor of some region or other, making sure there were record harvests to boast about on Radio Moscow in the days they seemed to mention nothing else on that station. You had a grandfather, too, who was sent into exile for failing to grow crops even though he had never been sent any seeds to plant to begin with. And there were also the years you spent as the driver of a combine harvester in the collective farm where your family lived, the time that earned you entrance into university, made sure you took your first steps towards that sparkling career you had.)

Yet to return to Alasdair, I splintered his heart that day, blasted it into tiny fragments with the way I refused to go out with him. And he reacted to all with dignity. A shrug of his shoulders. A sad twist to his lips.

'That's okay, Elizabeth. I had the feeling you might not.'

It was after that I met Andy. Distrusting him a little even that first time we met, he was a man who reacted very differently when I refused his request for a date. 'My dear Madam,' he declared, 'you are turning down the experience of a lifetime. A night in your life – and perhaps even more – you will look back on as one of the most sensational and unforgettable in your experience. Elizabeth, I ask you again, will you come out with me?'

This time I said yes.

Looking back, it is so easy to see why I was fooled. He was so different to Alasdair, a red-faced, dark-haired, untidy man whose feet were rarely rooted to the earth. Instead, they rolled upon the ocean, stepping on the decks of Merchant Navy ships that travelled across the Pacific, Atlantic, the Mediterranean Sea. He'd talk about them from time to time, either by my side or across the kitchen table from my father. 'Murmansk. Vladivostok. The Crimea. I've been to all these places,' he'd say, 'Poor bloody places. They all were. Poor bloody places.' And with words like these, he swept me up too, moving across the floor of the local hall, crooning songs into my ear.

'Calamine Lotion. It's good for the skin,' he'd sing, parodying the words of a Gaelic waltz. Or, 'Dance. Dance. Dance to the ten guitars.'

Yet I was swayed even more by the words of the other girls. They beamed every time he opened his mouth, laughing at his jokes, marveling at how far he had travelled.

'He's some man, that Andy,' they might say.

'I wouldn't mind a night or two with him, Liz. If only you hadn't got your mitts on him first.'

'God. You're a lucky, lucky woman.'

Sometimes, though, I'd catch his expression after we'd spent the weekend drinking and dancing with our usual crowd. I'd be aware of a darkness in his eyes, a look of desperation, as if all his wildness was an attempt to escape from himself, to evade the shadows that sometimes threatened to overwhelm him. There was one night he was sick after a party over in Maransay. His head was bowed, stomach retching, as he leaned against a wall.

'God,' he'd say, 'Elizabeth. I hate my Dad. The way he used to treat Mam. Always drinking. Wasting his money. And I'm scared that I might turn out that way. Don't let me, Elizabeth. Don't let me. You can stop me doing that. You're my protection. You're my wall …'

He stumbled then—the wall failing to keep him upright, his feet giving way. As I hauled him up again, he turned towards me, his eyes wet and tearful, mouth slobbering.

'You see too much, Elizabeth. You do. You see too much …'

No. I did not, Mikhail. At least not then. I didn't see the time that was coming for me, for him and us. He thought I'd be the saving of him. It turned out instead to be the wrecking of me, my children David and Michelle who turned their backs on our home as soon as they could. They had no time for the loop of drink and late nights that Andy coiled and fastened around our lives together. They wanted to escape the heat of his sudden rages, the coldness of the grudges – against his father, neighbours, even the English – he nursed within.

You, too, my dear Mikhail, must have suffered a similar blindness to my own. You failed, perhaps, to see the dangers in the white-haired, red-faced old man who clambered onto the turret of a tank in Moscow, telling them to turn around their wheels and drive away from the capital, that there could be no return to the bad old days of Brezhnev and Stalin, the old men who stood for hours in their Astrakhan hats on a balcony overlooking Red Square, watching the missiles roll by, troops strut past, the rifles on their shoulders, eyes forward, arms raised in salute.

You must have been grateful to him then. Boris Yeltsin. Saviour of perestroika, glasnost, the democratic experiment you began. Only to watch despairingly as that man betrayed you and others, the Red Flag you had known and loved all your days. Seen him, too, in his sudden, drunken rages. The moments he would stand in front of a band in a foreign capital and, waving a baton in his band, try his best to conduct them. The times when he would lie sprawled within the seat of an Aeroflot liner while a group of waiting politicians tapped their feet restlessly in front of a red carpet stretched out in front of an airport terminal.

I recall moments like these, too, happening in my life with Andy. The night he pretended to play lead guitar along with the Spectrums at a dance in Cairnbost Hall, asking them to play 'Your Cheating Heart' and 'Peigi A'Ghràidh'. The day he failed to turn up for Michelle's wedding, still drunk from the night before. The minister's feet tapping impatiently, clasping the Bible in his hand.

'Well, where is he? When is he going to turn up?'

On days like these I feel the same embarrassment you must have experienced the many times you watched that oaf disgrace the position you had honoured some years before. When I hear him stumbling through the doorway late at night, collapsing down the stairs he was trying his best to climb. Or the nights his hand is on the handle of my bedroom door, hammering away because, terrified of him, I have placed a chair tight against it. Hearing him yell.

'Let me in, woman! Why the hell don't you let me in?'

It's on nights like these, while I lie trembling and afraid, I think of what life might be like with other men. Those like you, Mikhail, or Alasdair. Those whom the world misunderstands and sometimes mistreats. Dismissing them as dull and boring. Condemning them for how right-minded and respectable they are, their decency and sense of duty, how the way they are so serious and considerate and kind seems to suck the very heart and soul out of them. And I blame all the rest of us for being far too aware of the tiny flaws and faults the world sees in such men. The red stains that blotch and mark their skin. The way they can be tedious and boring at times. The long dull conversations that might be found on the lips of those men who drive the likes of combine harvesters, diggers, tractors …

It's on nights like these, too, I dream of the likes of you, Mikhail Gorbachev, and long to have chosen your kind to lie by my side. It's on nights like these I dream.

With all my love at your time of loss and need,
Elizabeth

THE RED FLAG II

'It witnessed many a deed and vow
We must not change its colour now .'

1

Most days he worked upon his croft
he'd remove the layers of his shirt;
chest soiled by the stains and dirt
of peatbogs, soft

curls and wisps of hay,
or he'd sit behind his tractor wheel
in shorts, reveal
both sweep and sway

of muscle in his upper arms,
and speak of monumental plans,
of tunnelling through moorland,
both the threat and charm

of sea-eagles that he'd hoarded
to sweep above a neighbour's fields.
No. He'd never yield
to anyone. Not even on a village road

for as he declared on RT and Sputnik,
no normal rules applied to him.

Not even the Highway Code.

2

Some days he'd slip off soles,
imitating Khrushchev,
and keep the congregation under his control
by drumming on the pulpit

rhythms from the songs he'd known
way back in his past.
The Gaelic songs that flowed throughout his home
when he was young. The blast

of rock'n'roll or some pipe band.
And, too, that instant when his shoe
stilled in the fingers of his hand,
when that young woman once more came into view,

the one whose company and grace
had brought him peace and calm,
her kisses like soft prayers that healed the roughness of
    his face,
her voice the gentle rhythm of a psalm.

3

Shen's bedroom was the noisiest room
inside my childhood home.
Each hour the boom

of walking stick upon that upstairs floor
like a score or more
of bullets. The roar

of an explosion as he bayed
out for tea or coffee to be made.
We'd bring it up the stairs to him, afraid

he'd complain there was too much milk or sugar—
or not enough.
That the toast and marmalade was too tough
for his mouth to chew. We'd say nothing in response. Love

or fear preventing us from uttering a single word.
Until that morning came when we never heard
him. No rap on wood disturbed

us. It took an age for us to dare
to climb these stairs
to see if he was still there
with us. We halted at the bedroom door,
the silence more persistent than the roar
of his loud voice, wondering

if that blast and clatter was with us anymore.

THE LISTENERS

1

It was in the late sixties that the Open Presbyterian Church of Scotland (Perpetuating) decided to build a new Temperance Hotel for ministers and elders visiting Edinburgh. They consulted with architects and builders. It was one of the latter who suggested they construct it along Corstorphine Road with the building materials that they had developed for use in the Eastern European countries where their firm had been contracted occasionally, over the years, to work.

'We call it micro-concrete,' the man said.

'Well, what exactly is it?' the church administrator Murdo Macleod asked.

'It's our own brand-new mix. Fifty per.cent concrete. Fifty percent secret microphones, which we lace within the walls.'

The church administrator smiled, his eyes sparkling below eyebrows that resembled those of the Russian leader, Leonid Brezhnev, thunderous and dark, casting a shadow over everything he surveyed. Already he could see the value of these materials. They might go some way to prevent the splits and secessions, quarrels and disputes that had been plaguing their organisation over the last few years.

2

The church administrator used to sit for hours listening to the muffled conversations that took place in the

Temperance Hotel, surrounded by an array of warm grey coats, Homburg hats, and copies of the *Shorter Catechism and Westminster Confessions of Faith* with thick, embossed covers. He would listen out as much for doubts and hesitations as to what the ministers and elders on the floors below them actually said, conscious that this revealed more about what they thought than the avoidances and obfuscations which peppered their speech.

'You could tell what was on his mind by the way his words stumbled,' his favourite minister, also called Murdo Macleod, would say when he reported back on the theology of one of their newer colleagues, mentioning that the newcomer was not overly enthusiastic on the chaining of playground equipment in the children's park. 'He kept swinging back and forth on that issue,' Reverend Murdo might declare. 'One of his links to our church is clearly in danger of coming loose.'

If he was really concerned about the man's loyalties, he might have sent one of the elderly ministers from the remote islands where the church possessed many members, aware that in these places, members of the clergy were unlikely to be contaminated by any modern ideas and thoughts. The old minister would put on the Homburg hat and thick grey coat, the de rigeur black leather shoes, knowing these were all wired up and fit for the purpose they were intended. There were several recording devices lining his hatband, pockets, and collars of his coat, even a pair fixed within the heels of his footwear. He would begin to question the suspect individual on the important issues that affected the well-being of the church at that time, whether Scottish country dancing was a way of skipping lightly in the devil's footsteps or if the love of art – in any form – was the first shoe-shuffle in the direction of the idolatry that afflicted the Roman Catholic Church.

'What is your attitude to travelling on a ferry on a Sunday?' he might ask.

If there was the slightest pause or equivocation in the reply, the interrogator would press on with a further question.

'Would you step on that ferry if a family member was ill and in a hospital on the mainland?'

His gaze would be intense as he studied the man's face for the movement of his Adam's apple, a slight gulp of unease. There were times he even used to peel back his thick eyebrows in order to see him more clearly, his grin taking on the shape and outline of a sickle in his barely concealed desire to cut him down.

'Well?' he would say.

3

The Church administrator's work became more difficult in later years.

There were all sorts of signs and portents. There was the drop in sales of certain items. The Gospel Ship, complete with verses of Scripture that had been a favourite for decades disappeared, replaced instead by an array of family photos adorning mantlepieces. Photos of one of his predecessors, Reverend Morrison, with a thick dark moustache adorning his upper lip, a pipe clenched firmly in his mouth as he sat in the glow of a Sabbath sunset. So too, the unique Matryoshka dolls the Church had sold in its shops. There were two varieties. At the heart of one was the bearded, capped figure of John Calvin, looking darkly out at those who had bought the figures. Among those who enclosed him were John Knox and Thomas Chalmers, culminating in the image of the present Moderator of the Open Presbyterian Church (Perpetuating). The other looked more similar to its Russian prototype. A white-headed, black-scarved woman smiled benignly at those who had purchased it. Inside though, the same woman stared in a stern and judgmental manner as she clutched a whisky bottle, a pack of playing cards in her hand. In the final, smallest model, she was grinning again, holding a black-covered Bible in her fingers. For decades both these figures had sat on the mantlepieces and display cabinets of those who were the ministers of the Church. When one new clergyman was questioned about why he had not purchased this item, he shrugged his shoulders.

'My wife thinks they only collect dust.'

The Church administrator reacted with horror to this remark, repeating it endlessly to himself. Even when he dreamed, words would sometimes spill from his throat as he relived that conversation in his head, all too aware that they were not part of the liturgy of the kirk to which he belonged.

'Earth to earth, dust to dust, ashes to ashes ...'

And then there were the other changes, some of them involving the diet of many clergymen. The younger ministers no longer depended on their porridge in the morning. For years, the bottom of the plates from which they consumed their salt-laced cereals had been bugged, each early morning indiscretion recorded by the tiny microphone the bowls contained. (It was well known that certain members of the Church found it impossible to stifle their secrets each time they allowed loose a yawn, the former seeping out each time they opened their mouths.) Instead, they either ate toast and cheese or a plateful of Corn Flakes or Rice Krispies, the sound of their chewing muffling the sound of their sighs and voices.

There were also the ashtrays. Again the more elderly used them all the time, the hotel lounge clouded by smoke, a mountain of ash and cigarette butts growing nightly as the clergymen engaged in theological debate. This was not true of the younger ones. Together with the wearing of clerical collars and dark shirts, they had cast aside their cigarettes. One – a Reverend called Murdo Macleod, the fourth generation bearing that name – had taken to removing the ash-tray from the table where he and his colleagues enjoyed a discussion every evening. Each time he did so the waiter brought it back.

'There has to be an ashtray at this table,' the waiter whispered finally. 'The Church administrator wants it there.'

Murdo frowned when he said this, pushing the ashtray over till it balanced precariously at the edge of his table.

4

It was this moment that brought about the crisis in the church.

The young Reverend Murdo Macleod did something that would have been unthinkable years before. He tossed the ashtray from the table, watched it splinter against a nearby hard-backed chair. It was this that revealed the tiny microphone hidden in its base. With its loop and whirl of wires, it looked like one of the little black spiders they had often seen sprawling across the walls of the Temperance Hotel.

'It explains so much,' one Murdo Macleod declared, the red birthmark on his face darkening as he saw what lay before him.

'Like how I was talking to myself the other night, complaining about the lack of toilet paper in the room. Two moments later and the waiter appeared, a roll in his hand ...'

'Or how the Church administrator came up to me the other day, quoting the piece of text I was struggling to find in my private prayers ...'

'It all makes so much sense now.'

It was then the incident occurred that has gone down in church history as the 'singing revolution'. All the Reverend Murdo Macleods – and one Reverend Donald Macleod – standing together to sing a psalm. Something extraordinary happened when they reached Verse 10.

'The day and night upon its walls
Do go about it round.
There mischief is and sorrow there
In midst of it is found ...'

The micro-concrete from which the hotel was constructed began to crumble and collapse, the walls toppling as they collapsed across the city of Berlin a few years later, earth to earth, dust to dust, ashes to ashes.

THE TALE OF DONALD
*Reflections on the life of Soviet spy
Donald MacLean (1913-1983)*

*Who'd exchange the machair for the gulag,
the Little Minch's wonders for the icy Baltic Sea?
See the splendours of St Petersburg instead of Rùm or Jura?
Scramble across tundra instead of striding on Tiree?*

*And who would swap bagpipe for balalaika,
''Speed Bonny Boat' for the Volga's song?
Only the likes of our fair Donald,
the one who I loved but now is gone.*

*And I would give up the Caucasus and Urals,
Winter Palace and its pleasures for which so many yearn
just to glimpse fair Donald here among us,
just to see that lost one smiling when he at last returns.*

The diplomat and Russian spy Donald Duart Maclean was an individual with connections to the Isle of Tiree in Scotland's Inner Hebrides. His grandfather John Maclean left that island in the middle of the nineteenth century, moving to Haversfordwest in south-west Wales where he worked as a cordwainer, a shoemaker who made new shoes from new leather—as opposed to the cobbler who simply repaired people's footwear. He was a remarkable success at this trade. His sons also did well. Ewan who was born in Tiree became Chair of the British Medical Association. His younger brother Donald, father of a boy who shared the same first name, became the MP for Bath and – later – both Peebles and the North Division of Cornwall. He was leader of the Liberal Parliamentary Party from 1918 to 1920. During this period, he was Leader of the Opposition. Subsequently, he also served as the President of the Board of Education between 1931 and 1932.

Some aspects of Donald Senior's Tiree background remained with him, most notably his ability to speak Gaelic, his Christian faith and loyalty to the Presbyterian Church. His son Donald reacted against the latter, drinking excessively and rejecting the older man's beliefs, especially after his father passed away. Young Donald also was much more radical in terms of his politics, espousing Communist ideas and becoming a Soviet agent while studying at Trinity College, Cambridge—one of the later 'Cambridge Spies' which included Kim Philby, Anthony Blunt and Donald's drinking companion, Guy Burgess. He claimed to have left his Communist beliefs behind before he joined the Diplomatic Service in 1935. However, this was palpably untrue. During the following years, he worked in both London and Paris, passing information to the Russians while being employed in these areas. It was in the latter location that he met Melinda Marling whom he married on 10th June 1940, around the same time as German forces were approaching Paris.

Later he became First Secretary, working in the British Embassy in Washington from 1944 to 1948. This was followed by a period when he became Head of

Chancery in the British Embassy in Cairo, an important location at that point during the onset of the Cold War. It was while he was there that his drinking became more and more out of control.

Despite these issues, Maclean's career was not affected. He became Head of the American Department of the Foreign Office in London. It was at this point in his career that he fell under suspicion for his activities. This led to his flight – together with Guy Burgess – from Britain to the Soviet Union in May 1951. His presence in Moscow was not confirmed by the authorities there until February 1956.

Unlike Guy Burgess, Donald Maclean, after living in a rural cottage for several years, became a largely respected individual in the Soviet Union. Among other tasks, he taught English and worked for the Soviet Ministry of Foreign Affairs. (He also became highly critical of some aspects of Soviet life.) Through all of this, however, his drinking and abuse of his wife continued. Eventually she had an affair with Kim Philby and the couple separated. She later left Moscow in 1979 to return to the States. By this time, her relationship with Philby was also over.

Donald passed away from pneumonia in December 1982. The following year his ashes were secretly scattered one night on his parents' grave in Penn, Buckinghamshire.

The sequence of poems that follows is inspired by the life and the family and other connections of Donald Maclean. It, perhaps, should be noted that my grandfather was also a Maclean from Tiree who died many years before I was born. As far as I am aware, we are not related. However, as with other Macleans with roots in that island, such as the novelist Alistair Maclean and the Gaelic singer, comedian and writer, Norman Maclean, it is not impossible that there are loose connections ...

Childhood

1

Your father told you of a man who worked in Scarinish,
at the Temperance Hotel there, yet sold
whisky on the side, all wink-wink, hush-hush,
supplying a bottle or two of that gold
liquid to resident and guest
who'd come to take the air and waters of Tiree.

And you'd clearly been impressed
by that degree of subterfuge, the duplicity
and double-dealing, the quiet
offer of a dram—'*a wee deoch*'—
to those who wished to spend the night
fishing upon shore rocks or by a moonlit loch.

Years later you thought you were just like him.
The Cambridge graduate slipping secrets to the Reds.
The diplomat's artless indiscretions.
That Presbyterian conscience which led
to these dark betrayals of those who thought
were born within the fold.

Just like that man who slipped his secrets past the hotel's
     host
and offered guests a little sip of gold.

2

Your father, too, took family through the murk
and fog of London to Marylebone's kirk
in military formation, pausing to bark
out Presbyterianism's tenets,
how God had meant mankind for work
and worship, how they should never shirk
from duty. He never would have dreamt
of his son's betrayal or the breach of trust
that lurked in that child's future,
behind his spotless, ironed shirt,
and if he had, he would have condemned him
in language—brutal, damning, curt.

3

DONALD MACLEAN (1864-1932)
Father of Donald

He didn't feel he ever reached there,
like driftwood on the shoreline, Hebridean parvenu.
One of a cordwainer's brood who'd trekked south,
representing Bath and Peebles till the electorate threw

him out. And that feeling persisted
for all that honours came his way,
as his voice possessed the wrong inflection,
as if no matter how he tried, a trace remained

of his father's tongue.
And so he passed that onto his son
unknowingly—the sense he never quite belonged

4

GWENDOLEN MARGARET MACLEAN,
Nee DEVITT (1880-1962)
Mother of Donald

What under sway of heaven must have passed through
    Gwendolen's heart and mind
when she chose that man—nearly two decades older—
    to bind
and sleep within the matrimonial bed? And after she
    had married him, did she find
his Presbyterian mindset a force that confined
and constricted her? Oh, she must have been blind
when she picked the likes of him, her relatives decided
when they watched them at the altar—the silver-maned
    groom and his youthful bride,
hopes and aspirations swirling as their separate lives
    settled and aligned.

But as compensation, there were the clutch of boys
to whom she gave birth. She granted applause
to their small rebellions, the ardour with which she heard
    them raise voices
in argument, the righteous force of every youthful cause.

Especially Donald, her oldest son.
The one her husband struggled over,
finding him a puzzle, a conundrum,
wondering exactly where he'd end up
and from whereabouts he'd come.

5

Politics and faith. He'd sometimes overhear
Dad and Uncle Ewan in the drawing room downstairs
speak about the country, its troubles and affairs,
voices breaking off from time to time to bow down
    heads in prayer.

A form of worship too—the subject of their talks
sometimes blurred by Gaelic; at other times by Welsh,
but often concerning those who lay within a hospital bed
or found no release from hunger crouched at a school desk.

Donald would acknowledge this; the stature of the men
from whom he hailed, yet he still sometimes felt ashamed
of how Calvin and compromise always claimed them,
    how life remained the same
for those who said they'd help him, the streets and homes
    from where the desperate came

unchanged by their efforts—like Deuteronomy, believing
'*The poor never ceasing from the land,*'
with that Book's frail solution.
'*Thou shalt open wide thine hand.*'

6

Workers of the world unite, you have nothing to lose
    but the lash
of kelp, harsh upon your back; the smoke of pans
bubbling to bleach linen, create glass, soda, potash
to be fashioned from the ash of seaweed washed up on
    the sand.

Or so Grandmother told him, speaking of days
she'd left long behind her. He burned with the injustice
    that she'd seen.
How sores wept on the soles of shoeless men. The blaze
scorching eyes and nostrils. Winds gusting hard,
    relentless, mean.

7

On the fireside stool, two Bibles.
One thick, black and dog-eared from evenings she rifled
through its pages, seeking Gaelic psalms she might claim
comfort in. The other neater, more pristine—King James
Authorised, more rarely lifted, read.
And too, those pictures perched above her head.
The old man with his knotted, praying hands.
The Gospel Ship taking passengers to that land
from which there was no sure or safe return.

He wondered what she'd think of him, how he'd learned
texts from another gospel, quoting Karl,
Engels and Lenin, instead of Luke, Apostle Paul;
how his offspring with their crimson kerchiefs
had built a corner in their home where God and church
were set up to anticipate the hour in which faith would
    topple, fall.

8

*Donald's Grandmother Agnes MacMillan was a fluent
Gaelic speaker who lived in the family home for years.*

Sometimes fields and orchards would dissolve
and Gran would look out the windows of Elm Cottage,
seeing shades of Bailephuil and Sandaig
beyond Buckinghamshire walls.

The stretch of sand and machair;
pale silhouettes of mainland hills;
the ocean on her doorstep a ripple
through green foliage; Rùm and Eigg bare

on the far horizon. And she would babble
once again in Gaelic, exchanging news with friends
absent from that shoreline, exiled or having made their
        last descent
in Kirkapol accompanied by psalms, prayers and Bible

readings. In later life, he saw her as much more than kin
in the way she'd scour reports sent by island steamers,
seeking to work out what each scrawled line might mean.
All similar to his epistles to the Kremlin

where he sifted through the weight of every whisper
overheard at office door or corridor,
calculating what he might ignore
or what could signal threat or danger

to him as he negotiated rocks far more
deadly than those of which she'd told him many years before,
those outcrops that lost ships encountered
when they sailed close to Skerryvore.

9

He could sing in different voices
just like these calls that starlings made
perched on the roof
of the lightkeepers' homes at Hynish,
imitating sounds they heard in the hush
of sundown or the winds
swishing through a barley-field,
a rich, green crop of oats,

capturing the languages of others
somewhere deep within his throat,
mastering words
of other men the way these birds could mimic

songs of lark and corncrake,
gulls squabbling above boisterous seas,
as if he had been gifted wings
by ancestors passing on their skill for imitating tongues,

their ability to echo men and women
no matter whether they belonged
to Tiree, Wales, Cornwall, the Borders,
talk and speech breaching the divide

that formed barriers to most,
crossing mountain range and coastline,
till it seemed he'd misplaced
all sense of who he was,

and he could only find himself
within the talk of strangers,
far from the light men served in Hynish,
beam long obscured and lost.

Youth

10

Nights when seas were still and moon was full,
his father's people said that they could sometimes hear it,
these cries of anguish from the Ross of Mull
not that far from them, Ormaig, Shiaba, Kilvicheon,
these forgotten townships with their broken walls
the Duke of Argyll had burned down. And he'd blaze
        with the injustice
of each scorched and blackened stone—not like father
        who shut his eyes and called
these days a necessary cruelty, but as if these flames
        burned still,
embers smouldering within thatch, neither cooled nor
        chilled
by Atlantic storms, a force that tugged and pulled within
        him till
—like an earnest member of his clan—he longed to
        unfurl
the Red Flag, brandish it the way it flapped above the
        Clyde,
though he'd have to wait to do it, cool
his fury, complete the work he'd still to do in school.

11

*This poem contains a reference to Sorley Maclean – or
Somhairle MacGill-Eain – from Raasay who also
espoused Communist sympathies in his writing. This
ended when he became aware of how Poland had
suffered under Soviet rule. The following three poems
numbers 11-13 draw upon his work.*

He may too, like another member of his clan,
have quarrelled with his conscience as he walked
across the university courtyard, a beach, perhaps,
      or headland,
contemplating the hard extremity of Spain.

A miner trembling in proximity of horror. The slain
and wounded in mountains not unlike the Cuillins
his people watched from Tiree, imagining the pain
of those who'd made the choice

to serve that lasting cause.
But he put it from him, turning to the books
stacked upon his desk, not shouldering the cross
of his convictions. Yet he knew there would come a time

when that faith would summon once again to find
him prepared to follow it with courage and the sharpness
      of his mind.

12

Two men whose forbears hailed from close-lying isles
contemplating Spain:
one shifting gaze from Sgurr Alasdair
veiled by mist and rain
to see Barcelona under siege.
The other witnessing the pain
of Guernica as if it were Inverkeithing,
the battlefield where Clan Maclean
were cut and slaughtered.
Both aware that war and bloodshed
were veering mankind's way again.

13

His father told him to stay far from the forest,
for packs of wolves prowled there.

His father told him to stay far from the forest,
in case lone beasts might appear.

But he was always drawn to the forest,
despite the way he would sometimes hear

howling from the depths of the forest
and see the blood-stains, too, that smeared

the path twisting through the forest,
how it grew darker as his footsteps neared

the great house at the middle of the forest,
the rooms that all its subjects feared,

aware the wolves that stalked the forest
feasted daily in the shadows there.

14

KIM PHILBY (1912-88)
One of Donald MacLean's main collaborators

Kim spoke in Cambridge
of islands he once used to sketch,
each promontory, inlet, mountain range
imagined and set out on a page

in Father's study, shading with a pencil
the steep incline of countless Spyglass Hills,
stacks and skerries round a peninsula, the still
waters of a lake. He dreamed about this landscape till

its substance became real to him, something he could
      touch and see
when the choir sang, '*My soul, there is a country*',
envisaging dips and swells, each detail of topography
when they proclaimed the flower of peace, the sentry

that stood and guarded there.
He drew them in—Burgess and Maclean,
till that dream was their own and he'd gained
converts for the cause by speaking of the rose that
      cannot wither,
the slaughtered souls of Spain.

15

KITTY HARRIS (1899-1966)
Soviet secret agent and lover – at one time – of Donald
Maclean. Employed as a radio operator by the NKVD or the
People's Commissariat for Internal Affairs, she had a crucial
role in persuading him to work for the Soviet government.

Summer on that island, the thrum of bees.
Birds looping in and out of marram grass; their sharp blades
brought to these shores to withstand waves
that took storms and upheaval to the distant Hebrides.

Yet he found himself subjected to a different kind of assault.
The heady scent of perfume. Scarlet tip of lipstick.
Clips and nylon stockings. Underwear he longed to strip
so he might taste the sweetness of her flesh, the salt,

precious gift of blood. She provided all this; her presence
banishing all that was forbidden in Father's theology
till he heard songs that had been for centuries subdued,
        the rhapsody
of nature, the heady essence

of an Eden he wanted so much to believe in.
Its pillow-talk the virtues of the Reds,
the visions, too, she brought often to bed
combined with the heat and relish of what he'd been
        once taught a sin.

16

What brought you to the cause?

Oh, Grandmother's tales.
Her talk of equality and kinship among her fellow Gaels.
Perhaps, too, the fervour of her prayers.

And to what was this compared?

The grim dishonesties of that decade.
Misery and hunger. Men setting out from Jarrow on
    that cold crusade.

And all in contrast with?

How my pockets rang and rustled with loose notes and
    change.
How my shirts were pressed and ironed when theirs
    were crumpled, frayed.

And that's what drew you in?

All that. Some friends, too, seeking to persuade
with talk of injustice. They, too, shook and swayed
me to take up my secret trade.

So in its place, that dream?

Of red star over Kremlin,
beam rising from the tomb of Lenin
to bring a hint of scarlet
to machair, tundra, steppe,
wild stretches of the sea,
lighting up the stratosphere
from outer edge of Vladivostok to the Inner Hebrides.

17

Duart, the middle name that he was given
summed up the kind of man
his father hoped he'd be,
steadfast, loyal to the clan,
the Macleans of Tiree, Mull, Argyll,
'*Bas no beatha*', that sense of virtue, honour deep
within. How could he contemplate
the thought that his child would not keep
faith with ancestors, that he'd break free
of the ties and bonds of kin?
And all for this, those that bound men within the
    Lubyanka,
Stalin, Khrushchev, Beria, the flag that flapped bright
    and crimson
high above Red Square, walls of the Kremlin.

18

One day he was approached while on holiday in Berlin
by a young man in the Hitler Youth, recruiting, perhaps,
    for the Gestapo,
who asked him a favour—would he pose
for a photograph? They were looking for a specimen
of Aryan manhood, a perfect example of the German race—
tall, fair and blue eyed—and they saw him in that role
until he opened lips, consonants not quite right, vowels
slightly awry. Then there was that snarl upon his face.

'An Aryan?' he might have said. *'That test I fail,
I am a mongrel mixture of Anglo-Saxon, Gael ...'*

Work and Manhood

19

If Uncle Ewan knew about his nephew,
he would have dismissed his kin
as having read too much of philabeg and sgian dubh,
a brand of cloak and dagger set within

bracken, heather, glen and loch
—*Kidnapped, Rob Roy, The White Cockade*—
casting backward glances at those who lost
their final battle, the cause and leadership betrayed

like those who followed that red star
who always saw its lustre dimmed
by words and deeds of those who were in charge,
those shadows brooding deep within the dim lights
    of the Kremlin.

20

He sniffs the air, prepares his ground,
checks the level of attentiveness in those he sees around
him, listening to their rapidity of speech
when they meet or greet
him, measuring, too, how glacial are their eyes
and if there is any possibility they can see through
    that disguise:
shadows flitting on his face,
ears taut as he listens hard for speech out of sync or place.

It was just the same in Paris, Cairo, Washington.
An urban fox. Lupine metropolitan.
Scraping for hidden secrets, cachés, files
encountered in his working life. He travelled miles
since setting on that journey, testing each foothold
to see if it could keep him upright, through desert heat
    and Arctic cold,
attempting to ensure that traction could be found
and if the earth that held him contained solid, secure
    ground.

21

MELINDA MACLEAN (1916-2010)
Donald's wife, who also had Communist sympathies

Sometimes it is simple to render life invisible,
acquire a presence to which others
barely give a look or thought.
And so it was with you, the slightness of your frame,
the lightness of your voice,
no one had a notion of what you were about,
as you listened to the sages speak
inside Café de Flore,
heard exiles talk of how they fought
in Teruel, Girona, across the Pyrenees in Spain,
sipping coffee while they exchanged tales
of the hungry, wounded, the many thousands slain.

And this is what drew you to him too,
sensing there was more to him
than that towering bureaucrat some saw at first glance
till he blurted out his secret
one night you were together,
how his entire existence was a dance
between dim and distant partners,
a spin and quickstep as he sought
to further and advance

those whose cause had been defeated across the Pyrenees
    in Spain,
those still seeking justice
for the hungry, wounded, the many thousands slain.

And even when his kisses only left behind
a faint legacy of tenderness,
when he would choose
comfort in another's flesh,
or leave upon her body
the dark print of a blow,
the purple imprint of a bruise;
when she would scan columns to read tales
of show-trials, exile in Siberia
within the daily news,
all occurring among those who had been on their side
    in Spain,
now doling out injustice
to the hungry, wounded, the many thousands slain,

even then she would think it all worthwhile,
the agony, betrayals and the pain.

22

There were times when the island was a prison.
Grandmother used to reminisce,
recalling weeks when the steamer used to try and inch
its way towards the pier at Scarinish

and fail to harbour there.
Or else these days when the few boats seeking to fish
out of Tiree could not sail from land,
both wind and wave a mesh

trapping them on soil and sand.
But, hell, these days, his life was just like that,
a weather-eye straining to see the lash
of storm or shower darkening the horizon,

distrusting each hush
in conversations overheard in London,
Cairo, Washington,
anticipating jail or gulag in every wisp

of talk nearby or in far distance.
No chance either of some great ship
arriving at the quayside,
lowering its gangway,

allowing him to step free.
No. He had constructed his own prison
and he was locked and bolted
in a self-made quandary.

23

He would rustle through buff-coloured files
fastened tight with scarlet ribbons
in the way his father had sometimes read the Bible,
skimming from Genesis through to Revelations
to discover what apocalypse might come
if the stewardship of angels shifted guard
finding out the megatonnage of each bomb,
what battleships queued within their shipyards,
and then he would slip these sheets within his briefcase,
head out the embassy doors,
trying to avoid the piercing gaze
of colleagues, sentries, too, in uniform.

And this was his existence,
a constant dodge and dance
in which he tried to keep all others at a distance,
aware there would always be the chance
something might betray him.
A code broken by the spooks that sought him.
A microdot beneath a postage stamp.

24

He felt like Joseph there in Egypt,
as if, say, Potiphar's wife might soon see through
him, cry out the presence of a Hebrew
concealed within their midst.

And then there would come the cell
in which he—for decades—might find himself entombed.
No dreams or visions there, except for those hewn
by nightmare, seven years or more

in which he was imprisoned in his own private hell.

25

It was in Cairo he most often heard wolves baying for
    blood,
racing across desert, encircling pyramid and Sphinx.
He'd see the spoor of their paws, revealing where they'd
    trod and think

it would not be long before he was in their grip.
He'd smash mirrors to collect their shards,
try and repel them, rip
the underwear of others, guard
and shield himself with gallons of fiery drink.
But still there was that endless barking in the darkness,
howling in the distance, closing in
and pushing him towards the brink

of that time he might betray himself,
become less perplexing than the Sphinx.

26

(Perhaps, when he drank in Egypt,
it was his way of imitating the knack of embalming
that country's natives once practiced in the dark of tombs.
He'd immerse himself in alcohol, calming
nerves as frayed as ancient bandages wrapped
round cadavers. He'd bathe himself
in the protective heat of whisky, vodka, gin,
trusting each glass might preserve
the courage needed for acting out a role
that each day possessed the possibility of tearing soul apart,
knowing he might stumble soon like Karloff on his
*   unwinding path,*
aware that all which bound him would not protect or
*   guard his heart.)*

27

The Soviets called him Orphan
as if instinct, somehow, told
them he was a man bereft of bearings,
a spy needing to come in from the cold
and isolation felt among his peers
at Grisham. (The clenched fists. The jibes
aimed at outsiders, the dissidents
and misfits standing out among the tribe.)

But perhaps that loss went further back.
A foundling in a family shifting south.
The waif who found out he'd been born
with the wrong tongue in his mouth,

till each word seemed a betrayal
of a truth he'd hid within,
that all connections had been lost
to homeland, clan and kin.

28

There are different betrayals.
Sometimes he felt the sour
taste of his father's prayers and principles.
In these hours he swirled
the remnants of a whisky bottle down,
as if each drained glass
was tainted by his father's temperance,
recollections of a thousand 'Thou Shalt Nots'
shaping dark shadows in his thoughts.

His hand could stiffen into a fist
with which he might hit Melinda,
seeing in her countenance despair
that would have been within his father's face
if he had ever seen him
falling, reeling in forest path or city square …

29

A wave would break over him—a pounding self-disgust
as powerful as whitecaps hammering the coast
and he'd lose himself within it, within spume and surf
and lust for the flesh of others, never thinking there
    might be a cost
for him one day. Instead, he'd unhitch a stranger's skirt
or trousers, unbutton shirt or blouse
and guide them to a snare of blankets
where he would grip someone's shoulders tight, let loose
that storm inside himself, drum a creaking bed
and headboard with a grim precise percussion,
dig fingers deep into another's skin.

But there was no relief for him,
no sense of calm.
It was as if he was held in judgement by his father's
    prayers and psalms
for the host of treacheries that marked and scarred his life.
Infidelity to his country.
Betrayal of his wife.

30

The wolf often senses hunters.
The broken twig. A whispered word.
Swirl and shift of wind.
A scattering of birds.

Yet it wasn't that way for Maclean.
He was like those who revelled
in Bruegel's painting of the winter's chill,
unaware hunters were coming over the hill

towards them, cold, hunched,
empty-handed, half-ashamed
and looking down on that community
to find someone who might deserve the blame.

Flight

31

(i)

May 51. His own hour zero. The ferry to St Malo.
The moment he half-knew would come.
No bugle, siren, beating drum
alerting him. Just a whispered word, encrypted code
giving him a nudge and hint to go,
for all he'd long expected it.
Too many signs he'd been unable to dismiss.
His colleagues' glances. Files and reports
never landing on his desk.
He was all too conscious that the pack
would soon be hard upon them, breath hot upon his back,
their instinct strong to wound and kill
until that long drive to Southampton
with Guy settling down beside him,
the ghost of a school recital
a litany on his lips.

My soul there is a country
Far beyond the stars
Where stands a winged sentry
All skilful in the wars.

(ii)

And so they sped across the Continent,
over peaks and passes towards Berne,
foundlings orphaned by their actions
without hope or expectation to return

gu Lunnainn, Penn, neo Tir an Eòrna,
tir na gaisgich, tir mo ghràidh,
a' sgèith gu Moscow, troimh an cuirtean,
a' ruith bho ceartas, còmhla ri Guy.

What did they think, these two absconders,
aware who followed in their tracks,
conscious, too, there were no bye-ways,
no way or means of turning back

gu Lunnainn, Penn, neo Tir an Eòrna,
tir na gaisgich, tir mo ghràidh,
a' sgèith gu Moscow, troimh an cuirtean,
a' ruith bho ceartas, còmhla ri Guy.

(iii)

When he stepped down on the gangway,
the landscape lacked the contrast he long expected.
No divide into black and white. Just grim and specked
with rain. Much like the land he'd put away

from him. He'd anticipated some kind of revelation,
some confirmation that he'd done well and right,
but there was no sign of that. Just exhaustion after flight
across distance, the thought that he'd escaped the fury,
    indignation

of voices back at home. Even here,
there was no real welcome, only the cold response
of those who failed to comprehend how conscience
had led him down this path, the approach of an official
    who appeared

and placed a hand upon his shoulder, guiding
him to interrogation rooms, a place, perhaps, of safety,
    hiding.

(iv)

The interrogation reminded him of days
his father questioned him on his knowledge
of the catechism, the precepts of his Presbyterian faith,

a mindless recital of complex words
that held in common
the same dualistic vision of the world
as he found in *Das Kapital,*
new terms that replaced sanctification, justification,
the effectual call

'Convincing us of our sin of misery,'
the tight knots of his father's faith
transformed into this alien theology.

(v)

Burgess singing
the hour he was released.

*'If thou canst get but thither
There grows the flow'r of Peace,
The Rose that cannot wither,
Thy fortress and thy ease.'*

The Reaction in Tiree

32

Every village owns its small duplicities.
The shopkeeper whose finger tilts the scales
when serving quantities of sugar, tea
to those arriving in his village store. Dishonesties
of other kinds. The sailor taking off his ring
when visiting foreign ports. Or those who slipped
homewards with contraband stolen from their ships.
(Paint. Canvas from a sail. Cargo from the hold.)
And all for what? Cold distrust of others who placed
    them outside the fold
of trust? So it is with some living in small places.
Old dishonours follow them. Traces
haunting them throughout their days
even through the passing generations, fixed in the
    collective memory,
a permanent trace and marker within their DNA.

33

Saw corncrakes deserting fields of oats,
mating calls no longer hoarse within their throats.

Saw surf curl back in the distance, miles from land,
no longer melting deep in small ravines scored upon
the sand.

Saw seals slip from dark rocks into blue,
powering back down channels that they had just swum
through.

Saw the morning's sunrise decline to light the sky;
stars fade into darkness, turn off each gleam and die.

Yet no sights as strange as learning of a man from this isle
betraying his own people—bedeviled, lost, beguiled.

34

Most of their lives were tinged with brown.
Even the drove of hares lolloping round
the machair near stacks of kelp the tide slashed
down, the dun shade, too, of cattle cropping grass
winter winds had dulled,
heather hemming tight their world,
the peaks of Skye, Mull or Rùm.
Perhaps it was to escape that humdrum
shade they elected to see their lives in stark
divisions, a continual clash between white and black,
a mindset carried deep within the network of his veins.
And so, as his father had borne the stains
of sin and guilt and gone
each Sabbath day to Kirk in Marylebone,
he felt bowed by weight of privilege,
both boarding school and Cambridge,
that birthright he knew had not been given
to the people that he came from, those who still lived in
Moss, Vaul, Bailephetrish, those who still bunkered down
before the winds that lashed both high and low ground
on that island, those who gathered kelp upon the shoreline,
their fingers damp and coloured by the shade and weight
    of brown.

35

Relatives in their home, perhaps, in Caolas
must have rustled through the pages of the *Express* or *Mail*
to read tales of his betrayal
and discuss what might have gone amiss

with him. Perhaps they'd blame his English mother.
'She spoiled the lad.' She was not one of the clan
and they damned her for neglecting the skills required
        of a man
brought up on the island, claiming his sense of self was
        smothered

by being raised down south. 'The poor soul had no idea
        where he stood.'
And so they squabbled back and forth, quarrelling about
        ancestry,
the effects of exile, quite convinced he'd been
let down by the other side, that the Tiree part was whole
        and good,

just like them, those that for generations had withstood
storm and gale, and not been blown up on some foreign
        shore

like flotsam, wrack, driftwood.

36

Over time Tiree folk started to resent
the jests and laughter of residents of Coll
who pointed out Maclean's family connections
to those who lived, say, in Hynish or Balephuil.
They'd sigh and snort in quiet outrage,
knowing they were loyal in their souls
to those things that really mattered.
Christ, Church and the gospel.
The native tongue of these parts.
Their roots within this island deep
despite this unexpected squall.

37

'You should never build your house on sand,'
Dad used to preach,
yet he'd mention, too, how people
on the west side of Tiree scoured beaches

for flotsam, scraped canvases
and tea-chests clear of grains
of sand, lifted timber from the foreshore,
picked through the sea's tangle for the remains

of cargo that had drifted
towards Balemartin or Balinoe.
And with that they'd build houses
where they could cower and go

for shelter. They all seemed a bit like him
who'd built his home believing in the fullness of a tide
but now could sense it turning.
Perhaps it was just spray that blinded

men like him, Philby, Burgess.
Soon wave and wind would clear
and all the sand shift
from where he had thought to dig foundations,

lifting off into the distance
to reel and disappear.

38

During the Revolution, peasants heaved pianos
out of dacha doors and windows.

Hammers, pedals, keys, the belly
of the beast jettisoned in a cacophony

of notes, signaling discord
against those who for years had lorded

over their lives. And when he heard how piano wood
    and strings
tangled the flow of Russia's great rivers, he kept thinking

of how they'd treat that instrument in Scarinish.
Would his Presbyterian relatives have smashed

these same pianos, imagining the hands which
touched its keys were sullied by being rich

and privileged, their tinkle
of these ivories one more sign of how their souls were

surging downstream towards hell?

39

Is this what happens when some men waver
in their faith in Christ and God?

They become fickle,
seeking favour, instead,
from symbols.
The hammer, sickle,
red flag and stars,
Marx's fabled words.

So church-goers in Kirkapol
might have pondered,
seeing how the lives
of those who had left their shores
had been torn asunder
by one who had fled
from them,
but once broken bread
within their homes.

Russia

40

He thought of Tiree mariners,
beards spilling picture frames
like waves overflowing,
escaping places from which they came

years before—an island's confines,
a distant port or strand.
For he'd travelled farther than them
to reach this endless stretch of land

that only the Volga ever refreshed
with smoke choking Kuibyshev's streets,
grime edging into shirt-collars,
coal staining face and feet,

and where, instead of picture frames,
his expression shadowed by the flash
of front-page headlines,
both the clamour and hush

of public infamy.
So far had he come
to be greeted by questions of his hosts
who wondered why he had ever gone

on this journey, to be among
those who by
every word and action
made it clear he never would belong.

41

Clinking ice from the surface of the well,
he thought of how life sometimes swerved in circles,
imagining ancestors in Kilmoluaig or Kirkapol

undertaking the same tasks. Perhaps they might
have scoured the shore for driftwood, trying to keep alight
a slow and stubborn stove. Maybe, too, there were nights

in northern latitudes not far from Moscow
with the quiet talk of neighbours who'd only come to know
the limits of the Klyazma's flood and flow,

all not unlike—it seemed to him—the waves that washed
the shoreline of Tiree, though there were times he wished
for the lighthouse beam he'd seen in Hynish,

its pulse reminding him that life went on
somewhere beyond this landscape's endless hush.

42

His NKVD handler spoke continually of wolves,
how they were most vigilant in the dark of night;
could travel across mountains, relishing their heights;
step upon an ice-sheet, yet flourish in the full

heat of the desert sun.
Ethiopia. Alaska. Prairie. Taiga. Steppes.
He felt himself grow envious, aware of how he was kept
imprisoned in his dacha, distrusted, held at distance,

because of the service that he'd done.

43

Inter canem et lupum crepusculum

Between the dog and wolf, twilight,
that Latin phrase from Grisham he recalls during nights
when Klyazma is in the grim hold
of a polar vortex, its waters locked within cold
cataracts of ice on the river's surface,
heavy sky the shade of slate
that weighs down roofs at home.

Sometimes, then, he hears a wolf alone,
howling on the edge of forest, searching for her pack.
He wonders if there's some way back
for her, or if like him, there are boundaries of frost
and ice she cannot find her way across,
tree trunks, perhaps, hacked and split by snow
forming iron barriers on these twisting roads,
giving him and her no sense of where
they can hide or hope to go.

44

There was much they kept spick and spruce.
The underside of sickles
bright as crescent moons with stars
cascading loose down store-fronts.
Hammers forged on walls.
Stern statues of Engels, Marx,
in city squares and parks,

but much, too, that was an ill-fit.
Stout women with coats that split
and tore in winter.
The GUM store with its shelves
stockpiled with draughts and gusts.
Czar Nicholas still resident in the Kremlin
till sometimes he could hear the old priests stir within
to chant in voices like the songs
heard on Grandma's gramophone
when he was young
and made his choices,
when all he believed seemed sharp and bright
as those quarter-moons on store-fronts,
stars streaming through the Moscow nights,
when that Party-speak they scrawled
upon the sky at twilight
was full of the Gospel's certainties,
vibrant, unquestioned, bright.

45

Moscow State Circus. He was constantly surprised to see
so many memories played out there
by those poised upon high wire,
swooping up and down upon trapeze,
defying nerve and gravity as he had done for years.
Or leaping through a burning hoop unscathed
by flame, avoiding cuts of blades
when scimitars swirled, stepping safe and clear
from the tight confines of a box.
Yet most of all he saw himself in clowns
with layers of white-make up, fixed tears and frowns
painted on their features. He was Oleg Popov,
'*People's Artist of the USSR*',
Ivanusha, mime and juggler,
the face we peer into just to find
exactly who we are.

46

A drunken Saturday night. Guy picking out on piano keys
a long familiar hymn. *'My soul there is a country.'*
Maclean joining in to sing psalms recalled from
    childhood,
'O taste and see that God is good ...
I to the hills,' until he's back within that room
where Grandmother's eyes would fill with tears
remembering how she once looked up at Skye, North
    Uist, Rùm ...

47

There were nights when he'd see Burgess lurch and fall
in the vestibule of the Argavi, National, Metropol
or near the Patriarch's Pond where prostitutes might call
and hear the cold sneer of refusal,

and Donald wondered if he looked like him—possessed
        that shambling decay
shared by those who'd cheated and betrayed
the Motherland, those who thought they could up and
        leave, trade
nations, only to find out those who now surrounded
        them could sense the shades

and spirits of their former homeland in each sigh, look
        of disapproval,
their suspicions deep, unbending, primeval,
as if they could see through them, sense their inner
        unease and upheaval,
witness, too, the ghosts that spoke in reproof, accusing

them from cemeteries in Worthing, Norfolk, Kirkapol ...

48

Melinda gave her Judas kiss
to another who betrayed his land.
He watched her step away, take Kim's hand
and slip and stumble across the snow and ice

of Moscow, seeing her pass and fade
from his existence, recalling how she sacrificed
so much for him, the way she'd prised
herself from her own land, the high price paid

for all his treachery. He saw the cost of his deceit
in how she wrapped her arm around his former friend
and fellow-traitor, their years together slipping to an end,
while watching them in furs and Astrakhans risk that
      frozen street.

49

Was there ever a time of penitence,
when you bowed before your conscience or your God
and confessed your regrets at believing in this cause,
a moment you discovered, say, the weight of deaths

recorded among the souls that hungered in Ukraine?
Or how Beria raped these women agents harvested
    and reaped
from Moscow's streets? Or even earlier when the corpse
    found in the Seine
was found to be a dissident? What did you do to keep

away doubts and demons? Flail yourself with whips
    and chains
like a medieval flagellant? Drain dregs of wine
or whisky? Or instead of mortifying your own flesh,
did you direct your hate against Melinda, pounding
    time and time

again her body with fists till she bore wounds
that made her seem as if she had been impaled
like the Christ your father worshipped,
skin scourged and scratched by your clenched hands
    and nails.

50

By your bedside, Yuri Gagarin,
the picture of the cosmonaut who flew
and spanned infinities,
farther even than you,
seeing through the capsule window
the earth a flawless pearl of blue
glistening in black,

like the beam, perhaps, from Skerryvore
you'd glimpsed within
Grandmother's tales,
steady as a torch within your fingers
during these Arctic storms and gales
when blizzards beat and nailed
their chill into your flesh,
conscious that unlike the man who defeated space,
there was no turning back,

no prospect either of a spaceship
leaving a trail to blaze
the atmosphere,
returning him—with his kin—to these days
when their home was on a headland
overlooking beach or bay
near Scarinish or Sandaig,
where only soil or net might betray them
in the harvest of a crop or wave.

Return

51

Those Grandmothers known
in childhood might have laced
trailing pearlwort through the kirkyard gates
to stop the spirits of the dead from sneaking through

to their former haunts and days.
They didn't do that in Penn,
the Holy Trinity Church, for one night a group of men
slipped edgeways
through headstones, scattering MacLean's cinders
near his father's grave;
his remains a secret Red enclave
on which the other ghosts could look and wonder

why exactly a traitor's soul was now resting there.

52

After he died, it quickly became plain
spirits had passed on grandfather's soul,
and he imitated the long trek that cordwainer
took the summer evenings he strode

south to end up at the farthest edge of Wales.
But his grandson had a different journey. Heading east,
he sang snatches of the love-songs of the Gaels
overheard in childhood, turning silent when he reached

the outskirts of great cities—Leningrad, perhaps,
        or Tallinn—
his path meandering much more than the flight
he and Burgess embarked upon,
for all it wakened memories of what they did that night,

though no wall trapped him these hours.
Instead, his soul slipped over borders
without the beam of searchlights swirling from high towers,
without the Cold War chill becoming colder

when either side thought security was breached,
returning to the places from which his people hailed.
The family home in Penn. Balemartine's great, white beach.
A soft breeze in the Scottish Borders. A Hebridean gale.

The sweet calm of an evening after a life assailed.

53

Am falbh thu leam a rìbhinn òg
No'n téid thu leam thar saile
Gum faic thu ann gach nì gu d' mhiann
'S an eilean shiar a dh'fhàg mi.

Ged nach faic thu coill' no fiadh
Tha gèadh is eala bhàn ann
Cait' bheil sealladh a chuain shiar
Nuair bhios na liadhan traighte.

Chì thu uiseag agus smeòrach
Lon dubh agus luachran
Seillean ruadh le mhil 's a ghàradh
'S blàrag air gach buallan.

Chì thu sgairbh 'tigh'nn ort o'n chuan;
Tha lachaidh ruadh a' snamh ann;
Muran gorm a' fàs m' a bhruaich
Gach ceum mu 'n cuairt d' a' thraighean

Cha 'n fhaic thu nathair ann air grunnd
Ach luibhean 's cùbhraidh faileadh
A' cinntinn ann bho linn gu linn
'S an tìr 's an d'fhuair mi m' àrach

Will you go with me, my own true love?
Will go with me a distance?
To see all I long for far out west
In the little isle I once left.

No—you won't see forest or deer,
yet geese and white swans are found there
within the wide Atlantic's stretch
and when the tide lays sand bare.

You can see the lark and thrush,
honey-bees within the stone walls,
blackbird singing among rushes
fine cattle in their stalls.

The cormorant slipping deep in waves.
Brown duck afloat among them
Grass growing tall on steep braes
All around the shorelines.

No—you won't see snakes slither through grass
But sweet herbs and flowers
blossoming there for years and years
In the land where I was reared.

UNCLE DAN AND UNCLE JOE

1

Uncle Dan was going through his entire repertoire of songs as he drove us home on his bus to Lemresta. One moment, the choruses of 'Balaich an Iasgaich' and 'Eilean Fhraoich' were on his lips. The next, it was 'A Man's A Man for A' That' and 'The Red Flag'; the last sang so triumphantly that his voice was cracked and croaking by its end.

'It always makes me feel better, singing that.' He grinned, slipping his left hand from the wheel and clapping me on the shoulder. 'Restores my faith.'

I smiled back at him. For all that I was young, it had been easy to notice that for much of the last few weeks of our holiday, his mood had been as black as the tammy permanently fixed on top of his thick, grey hair. When he read the headlines in the paper, he'd groan and sigh, rolling up the sleeves of his thick, woollen geansaidh, fixing his thumbs in the pockets of his moleskin trousers and stamping around his home. He'd mutter to himself when he listened to the wireless, repeating the words 'Molotov' and 'Ribbentrop' as though they were swears. Worse, his huge, broad body would shake and eyes snarl when one of the village elders spoke.

'Looks like your old friend Uncle Joe has let us down, Dan. Sitting down with Adolf when Poland's on the table. Och, what else would you expect from a people who don't believe in God?'

These events, too, had kept Mam, my sister, Jessie Ann and me on the island. When we arrived at MacBrayne's office in Maransay, they had told us the 'Loch Ness' would not be leaving that day for Mallaig.

'We've been told not to sail.' The man behind the desk explained. 'At least for now. There's a chance that Adolf might send one of his big fish on a manhunt down the Minch.'

Mam fretted when she heard this, telling him about my father, alone and working in the shipyards in Glasgow. She had only come up for the summer because her own mother needed nursing. The boy, too, had to go back to his real school in Glasgow.

'Sorry.' The man kept repeating. 'Orders are orders.'

Uncle Dan stood at his younger sister's side, a wide smile on his unshaven face as she continued with her protests. 'It's safer here,' he grinned reassuringly. 'It would be no real hardship for them if they stayed here till the war was over.'

'Whose side are you on?' She glared at him impatiently, asking him a question that had been repeated all too often over the last few days.

He backed away. Yet from the look on his face, it was all too clear that he liked the idea of our family staying on the island over the next few months. He had all sorts of reasons for this – some he kept private, others not. For instance, he didn't like my father – something he made clear to me around twenty years later. ('The man's a lackey,' he told me, 'Giving all his wages to the brewery and the pub.') He also liked having Jessie Ann and me around. He and his wife – my Aunt Raonaid – had been trying for over twenty years to have children. And when we were in the village, we were 'his' by proxy. Our presence in his home cheered and strengthened him, bringing about a revolution in his mood.

'Oh, Uncle Joe won't turn his back on us for long,' he said to the next neighbour who teased him. 'He'll be back on our side yet.'

2

'You had a granduncle that was killed by Churchill. Alasdair he was called. Same name as yourself. The youngest of my father's family, the man was in the Dardanelles, the battle in the First World War that old Winston mucked up. The clown who now sits at Neville Chamberlain's right hand—you know what he did? He sent planes over the Turkish positions, more or less letting them know that the Allies were on their way. And, of course, when our lads arrived, the guns were there to greet them. That poor lad was like thousands of others. Didn't stand a chance.'

Dan stopped to place a moist kiss on my face, his cheek grizzled against mine as we gazed into a blaze that the winter's gales made necessary. Wind rattled the window. Rain drummed against glass. Their combined force gave his voice a greater intensity than ever, one that was accentuated by the constant movement of the hands that only spent a little of their time wrapped around me. One would stretch out, palm upward, to emphasise a point. Later, it would clench into a fist. There were other occasions, too, when it would move as if he were still controlling the bus he was paid by Murdie Campbell to drive between Lemresta and Maransay every day. Shifting its gears. Steering it right and left. The veins in his forearm rippling like seaweed as he turned the wheel or swirled his arm round in argument.

'That's possibly why the Russians let us down. They couldn't trust any government that had warmonger Winnie among its members. After all, he sent guns out against the railwaymen when they were on strike. Tanks were sent into that city where your father is now probably sitting enjoying his last pint of the evening.' He looked up at the clock on the mantelpiece, blinking as he noticed it was quarter to ten. 'A complete chancer. One minute he's writing articles praising Hitler. The next he's completely against him. That's probably why Stalin behaved the way he did. There's no reason to trust the likes of that man.'

And then he slipped his arm away from my waist.

'Anyway, it's time for your bed now,' he declared. 'You'd better get up there or Raonaid and your Mam will be onto us. And there's no stopping these women when they start.'

3

There were a couple of reasons why I stayed in my uncle's home.

There wasn't much room in my grandparents' one. An old blackhouse, my Mam and Jessie Ann slept together in a box-bed in a room that also served as the family sitting-room and kitchen. My grandparents occupied the room at the far end of the house, sleeping in separate beds since my Grandma had become ill the previous summer. Her coughs still punctuated day and night within its walls, summoning Mam to fuss around her, making sure she was comfortable. For this reason, she had little energy or time to speak when the two of us were together. There were none of the questions that had greeted me when I came home from school in Glasgow.

'What did you learn in school today? How did you get on?'

Uncle Dan's home more than made up for her silence. It was a 'white house'—one that been built from a mix of stone, a little cement, and a tarred roof just after the First World War. ('1924' read the inscription above its door. 'Two years before the Wall Street Crash came tumbling down on capitalists' heads,' Dan would say.. 'It won't be long before the whole shebang collapses on them again.') Despite its newness, there were problems with it. For all that Raonaid stoked its stove with peat every day, it wasn't as warm as the old blackhouses. Draughts whispered at its windows and whistled under its doors. There were no cattle in a byre that formed part of older buildings who could share their heat. Raonaid, however, supplied warmth in other ways. Her red hair as thick and bristling as thistle leaves, she met my entrance from school every day with questions she might have borrowed from Mam—and one or two she made up on her own.

'Did you learn a psalm today? What catechism did the teacher ask you to remember for tomorrow? What Bible story did you hear?'

There were times, too, when her fingers would hang loosely from the knitting needles she always seemed to carry with her and she would begin to tell stories of her own—tales of Moses and the Promised Land, the prospect of The Second Coming, how Christ performed His miracles even within our small community. She would tell these even to the 'duine dubh', the Pakistani who cycled once a month from Maransay with his case full of bargains, the coloured overalls and scarves that clothed Raonaid's round body for most of the year.

'You're a capitalist. You know that.' Dan would grin, watching him unfold his goods. 'The day will come when you'll be putting away that bicycle of yours for good.'

'Oh, yes, a' ghràidh. But until then, I have baragannan matha. Plenty good bargains.'

'Och, we know that. We see them every week,' Raonaid would interrupt. 'But what about your soul? Have you never heard of Jesus on your journeys?'

Dan would smile when she did this, only stopping her when she mentioned hell and the possibility of being burned in its undying flames.

'Och, you don't have to mention any of that nonsense. You want the poor man to be able to sleep.'

He wasn't as careful, however, with his own version of hell. Its torments would be recalled some days as he walked around the village with me by his side. He might talk then of the Great War, pointing out homes which had lost men on his way.

'Seamus Mackinnon used to live there. Killed in the Dardanelles … Iain A' Chantileer drowned when his ship went down in the North Sea … Stuffan's brother, Angus, killed in the last weeks of the war.'

He halted his bus one time near the end of the village where his own house stood—the border of the place everyone called 'Na Taighean Ura' or 'New Lemresta'. His arm began its usual flight. His fist clenching and unclenching on the driving wheel. His index finger jabbing in the direction of the houses, and then withdrawing once again, resting for a moment on the patch on the knee of his trousers. Tapping on the side window as though he were beating on a drum.

'See these houses …' he said, pointing at one and then another. 'They're all widows' houses. That's Seonag Meechie's.' He pointed at a 'white house' standing near the shore. 'Catriona Shoc's.' A jab in another direction. 'Murdag an Tarbh's.' Another point. 'Marissa's.' Jab. 'Every one of these was built for one reason. Each one of them, too, proved my father had been right before the war. You know what he said when the whole thing happened?'

'No …'.

'The minister had told us that if we volunteered to fight the Germans, we would get land for our homes. The Government had promised us that. Your Grandad stood up and told everyone in the kirk that if they gave us land, it would be the dead who'd build their houses on it. And he was right about that, for it was the widow's pension that paid for the first white houses that were built here.' His eyes bulged. 'Their men had paid for each stone with their lives.'

4

Other tales could only be told in darkness. Lying in my bed upstairs, I would hear them screamed out through the house. Moans and cries. An occasional phrase or sentence interrupting the peace of night.

'The bloody trench … It's falling in.'

'Iain's gone.'

'Why the hell have you forsaken me?'

The yelling would be followed by the sweet calmness of Raonaid's voice.

'Och, be quiet, Dan. It's all right now. Can't you see? It's all right now.'

5

There were moments, however, when there was no comfort to be found. The day, for instance, when news came that one of the village lads, Kenny Macdonald, had been killed. Drowned when his ship had been sunk somewhere near Gibraltar. His eyes red, mouth trembling, Dan sat slumped in his fireside chair. Big hands restless as ever, they switched from the bridge of his nose to the grey stubble on his chin, the back of his head to the inside of his thigh. He was a man wrestling, twisted and shaken by doubt.

'What the hell is that man Stalin playing at?' he asked.

Looking for answers, his eyes skirted the spines of the few books by the fireside. The verse of Robert Burns; the Bible; a pamphlet with the title, 'Why Spain Matters': his gaze fixed for a moment on them all. Raonaid peered across at him, her blue eyes full of concern.

'There's a greater Messiah than Uncle Joe, you know. One you can truly rely on.'

'Oh, eisd!' He shook himself – as if he were brushing away peat-dust from his clothes or the midges that clouded the island on a still summer evening – before sitting upright in his chair once more. His hands clenched into a fist.

'Let cowards flinch …'.

He muttered the words below his breath before he began to talk aloud again, speaking of people and events that I had never heard about before. John MacLean and Jimmy Maxton. Lenin and Rosa Luxemburg. Those who led the rent strikes in Glasgow. The naval mutiny at Invergordon. The unions on the Clyde. The men in the ranks, too, who had told him of such times and people. Keelies from Glasgow with the rich, red blood of Communism in their veins and its hard, clear thought in their heads.

'There was even one man there – a fellow, Mackenzie – who told me stories about my own people. Not just the Clearances, how the men from these parts were herded from these places and driven across the seas with their tails between their legs, but how our folk stood up against the landlords and sometimes even won battles against them. In places like Braes in Skye, parts of Ross-shire and Sutherland, even Aignish and Park on our own island where the people went out to claim their own land. The men of the Highland Land League who refused to pay the rent increases the estates tried to damn well squeeze from them. How they won the right to stay on their crofts with no man or power or police allowed to shift them …'

He would talk, too, of his own place in that history, his voice soft in the darkness, almost lulling me to sleep.

6

'After the war had ended, we waited for a long time to get the land the Government had promised. We wrote them letters, reminding them how they had said they would give us land when we all signed up. Homes fit for heroes. Instead, all we got were excuses. Delays. Long words fit for donkeys. Talk, too, of Lord Leverhulme who would give us jobs in town working the fishing instead of what we wanted, our own crofts and homes. Eventually, we decided we had heard enough bull. We didn't want to listen to their nonsense anymore.

'We broke into the farm at Lemresta one evening in spring, climbing over its boundary walls. We took some stones from it and began to build our own dykes. Just one thin line at first. Setting out the borders of our own crofts. Staking out our land. My good friend, Roddy, and me—the fellow who's now in Canada. We put up red flags where we planned to build our houses. Linen stained in sheep blood. And then, after a few words of prayer, a line or two of psalm, we began to plant a field of oats. Seed potatoes. A small crop of turnips. Our horses and ploughs turning up the soil there for the first time.

'The next morning, the ructions began. The farmer MacCulloch came to speak to us, telling me and my people that we were all thieves, stealing the land from others, even the stones from his wall. I told him that we had a damn sight more right to these stones than he had. It had been our ancestors who had placed them there—at a time when our people had been slaves to the tacksman. We had paid for each boulder with our sweat. Our flesh and blood and hunger. We had paid for them too on the battlefields of Europe, where so many of our people had died.

'He didn't know how to answer that. He stamped off and reported back to Leverhulme all that had happened, how these peasants had taken away the rocks from his wall and used them to build new homes for themselves. How they had defied him with their bloody red flags and their sheer bloody insolence.

'And after that, it was all lawyers and letters. Meetings in the village. Gatherings in the Town Hall. Where all the conchies of the day—the drapers, shopkeepers and fish-curers—had their say, sneering at us and calling us agitators and troublemakers and Reds. But me and mine just kept ignoring them. Taking care of the land. Using the stones from the farm boundary to build up our own walls. The dykes once made to keep us out are now what give us shelter for our crops.'

7

That evening, after he told me all of that, I went out and headed down the croft. A few wisps of clouds feathered out in a fan before the sun as it set in the sea out to our west, yet it was unable to hide its glory. Its light sparkled the ocean. It coloured, too, the field of oats I swished through with my fingers, scarlet tinting all that green. In the distance, I could hear all the noises of the beach: the whispers of its waves, the echoes of its endless, sourceless music, the soft splash against rocks. Birds whirled round me, their songs piercing and sweet. The wings of a pair of swans beat rhythmically across the sky, scissors of light snipping at the marvellous distances they travelled.

Standing behind their house, I could see Dan and Raonaid. He was crouched in front of a downstairs window, wearing his oldest and most patched dungarees as he dabbed white paint around its frame. He spent most of his evenings performing similar tasks throughout the summer, parking the bus beside his home and taking out a paint-brush, hammer and nails to make sure the building was both wind—and water-tight for the coming winter. Raonaid was out at the line, stretching on her tiptoes to take in the day's washing. A red scarf covering her head flapped in the wind. Dan had been the one to choose it from the duine dubh's offerings the previous week.

'It'll make you look like one of the Pioneers,' he had declared, lifting it from the battered suitcase. 'One of the defenders of the working class.'

'Och, eisd!' Raonaid laughed, flicking it in his direction.

Watching them at their work helped me to understand what my uncle believed in; how his faith had sustained him in the early days when he had first built his home. It had numbed him to pain as his fingers bled, placing stone after stone in the walls of his home, made him ignore, too, the flies and midges that clouded round him as he stacked manure and seaweed on soil that often seemed stubbornly barren, hoping to coax it into a rich and glorious harvest.

I sang his words for the first time, the way he must have done as he worked throughout the Twenties on this land;

'Though cowards flinch and traitors sneer,
We'll keep the red flag flying here ...'

8

On a June day in 1941, Uncle Dan's bus arrived at the house earlier than usual. He gave a yelp as his brakes screeched to a halt. Opening the driver's window, he shouted in my direction.

'The Nazis have turned on Russia! Uncle Joe's back on our side!'

He danced across the kitchen floor, spinning me, Raonaid, and my little sister to the rhythms of some imaginary reels that were swirling through his head. A cod's head, perched on the edge of a plate in the middle of the kitchen table, gaped at us in bewildered surprise. Its wide eyes seemed to follow us as we moved around the room, listening to him chanting the choruses and verses of a strange collection of songs—ranging from puirt a'beul to 'Scots Wha Hae', Gaelic songs of sadness and exile to 'Rule Britannia'. The last song sounded odd upon his lips—as if someone whose only loyalty had been to Russia and the working classes had been transformed by events into a flag-draped patriot.

'We're going to win the war now! We're going to win the war!'

We all gaped in surprise at what he did next, opening the kitchen and taking out a bottle of Johnny Walker. He splashed some of this into two of the household's cups, handing one to Raonaid when he had finished.

'To the revolution,' he declared.

She looked at her drink cautiously before putting it to her lips. 'To the revolution,' she grinned, winking in my direction

An hour or so later, he was sitting in his chair, his hands fluttering once again. They shifted from his stockinged feet to the back of his head, the patches on the knees of his dungarees to the arms of his chair. They were never still or rested.

'I thought Stalin had betrayed us. Standing side by side with those who had bombed Guernica. Shoulder to shoulder with the ones who had turned their guns on the people of Abyssinia.' He shook his head, his fingers tapping. 'I nearly lost my faith. I nearly started believing all these kirk elders and hypocrites who kept telling me that the Soviets were nothing but a bunch of devious atheists who couldn't be trusted or believed.'

He reached for the scone that Raonaid had prepared for him, its surface coated with a thick covering of crowdie and cream. He swallowed a mouthful. Trembling as he choked it down, his eyes watered.

'Well, I don't know exactly what Uncle Joe was playing at. I can't figure that out at all. But we'll see now exactly where the Russians stand. If anyone is going to stop Adolf, I have a good idea who that's going to be.'

And then, just before we went to bed, his favourite song—'A Man's A Man For A' That'—came to his lips. His voice was strong as the words rang out over both his own home and the community – 'New Lemresta' – that he and his fellow raiders had created within the now invisible borders of the old farm.

Raonaid wept as he watched him. 'He's back to his old self.' She smiled. 'At long last, he's in his usual.'

9

A tangle of memories.

The household listening to accounts of El Alamein and Stalingrad on the wireless. Reading news reports of battles won and lost. Shaking the hands of those who had lost sons, husbands or brothers. Greeting those who became married when their men were home on leave. Going to baptisms of children whose fathers were months and miles away. Watching funerals from the kitchen window where the family's men were absent from the long processions carrying the coffin to the grave.

The whole surge and fall of life's experiences. Tears and smiles. Fear and hope. Frowns and laughter. The ordinary, everyday labours too. Taking in harvests of hay, oats, potatoes. Planting crops behind the plough. Feeding cattle and sheep. Watching ewes give birth. Helping with calving. The village-men, too, working in the peats. Cutting and gathering. Bringing them home in ancient lorries, trailers tugged by tractors, even horse and cart. Heading out in the village boat, too, to do some fishing.

Tormod and Iain – two boys my own age – sitting at the stern with their toes in the water. Uncle Dan and the others rowing. Me perched at the prow, feet dangling overboard. The surface of the water almost still as the oars creaked and splashed, making our way past the rocky crags not far from the village quay. On one of them, as we passed close by, some seals were basking. They stared at us, confused by our presence, for a long time failing to move until their instincts overcame curiosity. They slithered over seaweed into water, splashing as they did so.

'Hard to believe there's a war going on,,' Dan said.

And then he began to talk about what might happen when it was all over; how the days of the rich lying back and basking while the working class sweated and toiled were over, how the genius of Uncle Joe would be recognised even by those who derided and mocked him, how Communism would govern within these shores.

'At long last, there'll be justice for ordinary people. Proper schooling for our children. Decent hospitals for the sick. More control over our lives. Slipping out from under the thumbs of those who've kept us down for long enough. Where we've lain and rotted for too many years.'

10

We waited at the pier when the war was finally over, watching as the steamer coughed and smoked its way into Maransay. A man with an anchor tattooed on his right arm passed us. A cluster of herring dangled from a string in his fingers, line threaded through their gills. Its silver glinted, even in the dull light of the afternoon.

'Glory to the heroes of Stalingrad,,' the man smiled across at Dan.

'Glory ...' my uncle replied, grinning quietly in response.

He was barely in control of his feelings, shaking as he held my sister Jessie Ann's hand. He had even shaved, something he only did on Saturday night, and slipped on a collar and tie for the occasion. ('It makes me look like a bloody bourgeois,' he had complained when Raonaid thrust it in his direction.) It added to his stiff and awkward look as he watched the steamer move close, slowing till its hawsers could be tossed to shore and tied. The gangway was rolled into place, stretching out like a drawbridge to the front gate of a castle. The harsh peal of metal could be heard all around the quay, almost the final note of our lives there as it clanged upon concrete.

'Well, that's it ...' he muttered.

Both he and Raonaid pressed stern kisses on our cheeks and coins into our hands. He walked away, moving into the huddle of people who had also come to the quayside to see relatives either visiting or leaving home. He circled round a thin man in tweeds who talked excitedly about the week he had planned 'fishing at the Lodge', looking him up and down in disdain. He passed an old woman in Sunday black who was weeping loudly as she waved in the direction of the boat. And then there was no sign of him. He disappeared into the middle of a group who were smiling and hugging and slapping the backs of their friends and loved ones.

'Where is he?' I asked Jessie Ann.

'Don't know.'

'He's gone home. I know he's gone home.'

And then he was in sight once again. It was easy to spot him on the quayside as the 'Loch Ness' piped off our departure. His hand was the only one clenched in salute as the boat moved away from the harbour. Triumphantly, he brandished it above everyone's heads.

11

I didn't see much of him after that.

There were letters, though, from Raonaid which Mam read aloud in the flat. The words would echo in the silence while we sat around the fireside waiting for Dad to come home, taking us back to the island we had left a short time before.

'According to Dan even the hens are laying more eggs and the cows giving more milk since Mr Attlee came to power though of course he's not going far enough, not squeezing the life out of the rich the way he'd like to see them do, there is a chance he might turn into another Ramsay MacDonald, a traitor to the working classes or so Dan thinks, the man is not a patch on his old favourite, Uncle Joe.'

A rare laugh came to Mam's lips.

'So like my brother. So like the man.'

Her words sparked a thousand stories from her memory: how Dan had stuffed a bar of Port Sunlight soap down the mouth of a bank-clerk who had asked him what he was doing spoiling Lord Leverhulme's plans by raiding Lemresta farm; how he told the minister that after the Revolution came, they'd find a better use for his collar; how he'd placed an old hammer and sickle into the fishing bag of an aristocratic angler who had used his bus for transporting him to and from a loch for a fortnight. Mam's eyes glittered as she recounted these tales again and again, forgetting for a short time the cold-eyed drunkard who stumbled home from the shipyard to her home every night.

There was another letter I remembered reading five-or-so years later which told of Dan's reaction when Churchill had been elected into power once again. He had taken to his bed for days, lying wrapped up in his blankets and refusing to drive the bus to town. ('If that's what the working classes want,' he announced, 'let them keep the chains around their ankles, the blisters on their toes. I'll not ferry them back and fore.') He was only persuaded to return to work after Raonaid convinced him that it was only the working classes between Lemresta and Maransay he was affecting by his actions. ('And they don't count for much in the grand scheme of things.')

After that, there was less talk of politics. A few muttered words of contempt about 'Winnie the windbag' whenever Churchill was heard on the wireless. A sigh or shake of the head when there were reports of Stalin turning his guns on the people of Hungary or some other part of the Soviet Empire. ('Oh, Uncle Joe … What the hell are you doing now?') Over the years, Dan became a smaller and slighter presence in my life—a process hastened by the fact I only spent a couple of weeks in his company each year. An occasional fortnight's holiday. A visit to the graveyard where it seemed with every passing season, more and more of my relatives were taking up a greater share of the available space. Grandma, Grandad, Raonaid, Dan, even my own mother and father: they all eventually occupied their own section among its sandy soil and granite headstones. My head was bowed for each of them as the minister's words blew away on the wind that seemed a constant presence there.

'Man that is born of a woman is of few days, and full of trouble. He cometh forth like a flower, and is cut down: he fleeeth also as a shadow, and continueth not …'

Yet it was at another kind of funeral that I thought about Dan most of all. I watched the Berlin Wall come down as some of my grandchildren clustered round me. They were playing on little electronic handsets that bleeped as the small planes they controlled dipped and dived above the guns ranged in their direction, trying to put an end to their flight. For all their efforts, the young ones were winning; their bombs and missiles destroying the wall of artillery below.

'Wheesht! There's something important on the telly!'

They didn't listen, intent on their own explosions and the whine of shells. I focused on the TV screen alone, straining to hearing the commentary. A young man was swinging his pick at concrete, creating a hail of grey and white dust each time his blow broke through.

Another danced on the ridge at its summit, reaching out a hand to pull his partner up beside him. The two reeled drunkenly, the young girl's red hair fanning her face while an East German guard looked on. He seemed much the same as MacCulloch must have been on the day Dan and his friends broke through the boundary of his farm—lost and confused, wondering how and when the rules had been changed and what he was supposed to do now they had been.

And all around them, there were those who were picking up pieces of the wall, chunks of concrete that might sit upon their window ledges, bookshelves, mantlepieces or, perhaps, be incorporated into the boundaries of their own homes or gardens. A small souvenir of the great changes that had come about in their lives, it would help to form the new borders of their existence, markers by which they could, if chance or fate allowed it, learn to live out the remainder of their days.

STALIN MO RUIN-SA

Stalin mo rùin-sa is Lenin mo ghràidh
Ainnir mo chridh-sa 's i Khrushchev mo dhàin
Tha m'inntinn làn Soviet bhith tilleadh gun dàil
Gu Stalin mo rùin-sa is Lenin mo gràidh

(Traditional Gaelic song, slightly adapted)

NOTES

THE BOOK OF DONALD

Poems 11, 12 draw their inspiration from *Dàin do Eimhir* by Sorley Maclean. He also drew on the image of wolves in his work. (13).

Poem 53 is a Tiree love song. Known as the Tiree Bridal Song, it was originally composed by Alexander Sinclair (Alasdair Nèill Òig), a Glasgow wine merchant.

For this sequence of poems, I owe a tremendous debt to the following books:

A Spy Named Orphan, Roland Philips. (Bodley Head)

A Divided Life, Robert Cecil (Thistle)

A Spy Among Friends: Philby and the Great Betrayal, Ben Macintyre (Bloomsbury)

I would also like to acknowledge my debt to Wayne Price, Hugh MacMillan, Ken Cockburn, Donald Meek for their support and encouragement in this.

SONG FOR A TSAR

Though it is rumoured that Catherine Mackinnon was buried in Russia and that Alexander I sang at her funeral, this is not true. Having passed away in Italy, her body can be found in the English Cemetery in Florence.

PREVIOUS PUBLICATIONS

Versions of some of the poetry and prose published in this book have been published in various editions of *Northwords Now*, *New Writing Scotland*, *Southlight (Dumfries and Galloway)*, *Causeway/Cabhsair*, *Gutter*, and *Southlight*. I would like to apologise to any magazines and other publications I have omitted from the above. While most of the work in this book is published here for the first time, there are a few poems that first appeared over twenty years ago.

THANKS

I would also like to thank John Joe MacNeil for his quick glance over the Gaelic spelling. (I have to take responsibility for any mistakes, especially for the songs included in the book.)